UNDERSTANDING
ANITA BROOKNER

Understanding Contemporary British Literature
Matthew J. Bruccoli, Series Editor

UNDERSTANDING
Anita
BROOKNER

Cheryl Alexander Malcolm

University of South Carolina Press

Published in Columbia, South Carolina, by the
University of South Carolina Press

Manufactured in the United States of America

06 05 04 03 02   5 4 3 2 1

Library of Congress Cataloging-in-Publication Data

Malcolm, Cheryl Alexander.
  Understanding Anita Brookner / Cheryl Alexander Malcolm.
    p. cm. — (Understanding contemporary British literature)
  Includes bibliographical references (p.   ) and index.
  ISBN 1-57003-435-4 (cloth : alk. paper)
  1. Brookner, Anita—Criticism and interpretation. 2. Women and
  literature—England—History—20th century. I. Title. II. Series.
  PR6052.R5816 Z78 2001
  823'.914—dc21   2001003344

For David

CONTENTS

EDITOR'S PREFACE

The volumes of *Understanding Contemporary British Literature* have been planned as guides or companions for students as well as good nonacademic readers. The editor and publisher perceive a need for these volumes because much of the influential contemporary literature makes special demands. Uninitiated readers encounter difficulty in approaching works that depart from the traditional forms and techniques of prose and poetry. Literature relies on conventions, but the conventions keep evolving; new writers form their own conventions—which in time may become familiar. Put simply, *UCBL* provides instruction in how to read certain contemporary writers—identifying and explicating their material, themes, use of language, point of view, structures, symbolism, and responses to experience.

The word *understanding* in the titles was deliberately chosen. Many willing readers lack an adequate understanding of how contemporary literature works; that is, what the author is attempting to express and the means by which it is conveyed. Although the criticism and analysis in the series have been aimed at a level of general accessibility, these introductory volumes are meant to be applied in conjunction with the works they cover. They do not provide a substitute for the works and authors they introduce, but rather prepare the reader for more profitable literary experiences.

M. J. B.

ACKNOWLEDGMENTS

For their assistance at various stages in the preparation and writing of this book, I thank Gerald Jacobs and Sue Greenberg of the *Jewish Chronicle* in London, and Robert E. Hosmer, Jr., of Smith College. I thank the editorial staff of the University of South Carolina Press for their skillful work on the book. The gratitude of a lifetime goes to my sisters, Ginny, Hope, and Joan, and to my godmother, Mary Miserlis. I thank my husband, David, without whose support none of this would have been possible. To my sons, William and James, my thanks as well as always.

CHAPTER ONE

UNDERSTANDING
ANITA BROOKNER

Understanding
Anita Brookner

Anita Brookner is a native Londoner. Apart from three years in Paris, she has lived in London all of her life yet admits she has "never been at home, completely."[1] Displacement, which is so much an aspect of her characters' lives, is something she learned of firsthand from childhood. The only child of Polish Jews, she grew up in an extended household of relatives and friends, many of whom had fled the Holocaust. Born on July 16, 1928, to Newsom and Maude (Schiska) Bruckner, who changed their name to *Brookner* in response to anti-German feelings in Britain ("Like calling yourself Batehoven!" she says), she was brought up Jewish but, never having learned Hebrew, regrets that she could never "join in fully."[2] Feelings of being displaced in some measure from her Jewishness are echoed in interviews where she confesses to having no religious faith but wishing she had. A sense of being a part of two cultures—but also *apart*—was clearly the legacy of Brookner's family. She describes her maternal grandfather as having "adopted every English mode that he could find" but for whom "European habits of thought—melancholy, introspection—persisted."[3] The combination according to Brookner was anything but a positive one. Even Brookner's father, who set her to reading Dickens from the age of seven, "remained very Polish" to her.[4]

Brookner's maternal grandfather immigrated to England at the end of the nineteenth century. Her father immigrated just before World War I. The melancholy that permeated the household in which Brookner grew up had possibly as much to do with the temperaments and trials (particularly of illness) of its members as with their reception in England. Brookner never writes specifically about anti-Semitism but does deal symbolically with the subject of conversion. *Look at Me* (1983) presents the most developed treatment of this and related issues of loyalty and collective identity through the story of a lonely woman befriended by an upper-class English couple who try to convert her to their hedonistic ways. Although Brookner does not speak of anti-Semitism as such, in interviews she does refer to "the English" as separate and different from herself. The "us and them" polarity she uses on these occasions is in itself very revealing, suggesting confrontation and opposition or, at the least, the divide separating outsiders from insiders.

Brookner is as noncommittal about exactly where her Polish roots lie as she has been evasive at times about her age. What she does say is supported by her more autobiographical novels. Relatives on her mother's side, for instance, had been well-off entrepreneurs. In their case, England did not offer the opportunity to find work so much as to continue businesses. In the family chronicle *Family and Friends* (1985), which was inspired by an actual photograph of Brookner's family, this is just what happens. Here, as in *The Debut* (1981) and *Latecomers* (1988), the protagonist's background is German. In *Hotel du Lac* (1984) and *Dolly* (1993), family roots go back to Vienna at the beginning of the century. Although these settings might seem at variance with anything autobiographical, given Brookner's professed Polish origins, they are considerably more than mere backdrops randomly picked off a map of continental Europe. In fact, the Jewishness of characters serves to link these origins to Brookner's own.

Brookner's father came to Britain at the age of sixteen, served in the British army during World War I, then went on to work in the

Schiska family's tobacco factory, where he was to meet Brookner's mother, Maude. At one point in his life, he changed his first name to Newsom. As in real life, name changes in Brookner's novels generally do not succeed in transforming characters any more than they succeed in turning them from outsiders into insiders. Closest to her father's experience of Anglicizing a name too difficult for the English to pronounce is that of Mrs. Miller in *Altered States* (1993). She changes her Polish name of Jadwiga to Jenny but still lingers on the margins of a family and culture not her own. Another example is the father in *The Debut* (1981). Like Brookner's own father, he is foreign born, but is German, not Polish. With his mother he is "Georg." With his English wife he is the more easily pronounceable "George." The implication is that he moves between two worlds. Brookner parallels name changes with a desire for leaving and entering other worlds to perhaps the best effect in *Providence* (1985). Here, the protagonist goes by the name Kitty Maule with her English university colleagues and by that of Therese with her foreign born grandparents. The result however is that she feels fully at home with neither. Similarly in *Hotel du Lac* (1984), the protagonist has two names, a given name and an adopted pseudonym representing the actual and fictional worlds between which she moves. When her real-life German middle name of Johanna draws the attention of a Swiss hotel clerk, the suggestion is that she does not fit precisely in either somehow. "An unusual name for an English lady. Perhaps not entirely English. Perhaps not entirely a lady. Recommended, of course. But in this business one never knew," he ruminates.[5] As a symbol for belonging, whether real or wished for, names and name changing feature repeatedly in Brookner's writing.

Maude Schiska, although born in England, provided an example of displacement in another form. Marriage and motherhood spelled the end of what had been Schiska's professional singing career, an experience that left her "inclined to melancholy" broken only by passionate outbursts of song.[6] According to Brookner, this was a major source of conflict between her parents and one that made her conclude that her mother, not herself, "should have been the liberated woman."[7] While most obviously the model for the excitable and frustrated actress mother in her first novel *The Debut* (1981) and, to a lesser extent, for the radio singer Fay who trades her career for marriage in *Brief Lives* (1990), the disappointment that Maude Schiska felt clearly made its impact on her daughter and can be viewed as the template for a steady stream of characters, especially female, whose lives fail to live up to expectations.

Brookner's own life, however, reads like a success story—or even two of them. The first of these is her rise in the world of academic art history. Before ever setting out to write a novel, Brookner was a writer and translator in the area of art history for two decades. A specialist in eighteenth- and nineteenth-century French art, her contributions to this field of study established her as an international authority. Among her publications were studies of J. A. Dominique Ingres (1965), Watteau (1968), Diderot, Stendhal, Baudelaire, Zola, the brothers Goncourt, and Huysmans under the collective title *The Genius of the Future* (1971), and Greuze in *Greuze: The Rise and Fall of an Eighteenth-Century Phenomenon* (1972). This last study grew out of her doctoral dissertation, which she researched for three years in Paris with the support of a French government scholarship. This period abroad would provide her with a setting for her novels which features, if not with as much frequency, with as much importance as London. Paris would come to represent freedom from filial obligation, an end to deferred pleasure, the beginning of a sense of belonging, and the possibility of a fresh start; this is the antithesis of everything that London would be made to represent in her novels. Conversely, Brookner's Paris is more of an ideal than any actual city. Notwithstanding this, its positive features closely resemble those real-life ones that attracted many of America's "Lost Generation" of expatriate artists, writers, and musicians. The circumstances under which Brookner returned to London could not have helped coloring her view of both cities. It certainly provided the material for her first novel, in which a young woman studying French Romanticism embarks on an independent life for herself in Paris only to have to return to London at its outset. Neither Ruth Weiss in *The Debut* (1981) nor Brookner herself would ever return to live in this city of dreams. What puts an end to their voluntary exile is a call from home. The model for the dutiful daughter who puts family first at considerable cost to herself is of course Brookner.

After returning to London to care for her ill parents, Brookner would maintain her ties to France through her work as a translator and a novelist. In the years to come, books on such subjects as Utrillo, the Fauves, and Gauguin would be made accessible to an English readership through Brookner's facility for rendering French into English and ability to write with sophistication yet seeming ease. Meanwhile, French settings, literature, and the cadences of the language would find a place in many of her novels, returning her, as circumstances could not, to that place that promised an altogether different future from what fate handed her.

On January 30, 1974, Brookner stood before members of the British Academy and delivered a lecture on the eighteenth-century

French painter Jacques-Louis David. When she wrote *Providence* eight years later, she would make a lecture of similar importance a symbol for the ironies in a rising young academic's life. Although Kitty's lecture is on literature, not art, like Brookner's it concerns French Romanticism. Also like Brookner's, it marks a rite of passage in academia and shows her to be accomplished and as witty as she is elegant. Yet this is only half the climax of *Providence*. The other is Kitty's barred entree into a kitchen. When the host of her celebratory dinner emerges with a soup tureen and a student aptly named Fairchild, Kitty learns that for all her success at work she is a failure in love. One offers no compensation for the other.

Brookner says that all she ever wished for were six sons. The implication is that no number of accolades can compensate for a lack of family. In the absence of children, Brookner devoted her energies to teaching and writing. Devotion, which is so much an attribute of her protagonists, has clearly been directed onto her work since the loss of her parents. *Jacques-Louis David* (1980) took her ten years to write, nearly as long as she spent caring for her parents. Both experiences took their toll. By 1985, she would say she had lost "the energy and perhaps the belief" to write a major art history study again.[8]

The story of Brookner's literary career begins in the summer of 1980 when she was on vacation from teaching at the Courtauld Institute. "It was most undramatic," she explains. "I just wrote a page, the first page, and nobody seemed to think it was wrong. . . . So I wrote another page, and another, and at the end of the summer, I had a story."[9] The story she wrote was *The Debut*. At a time when others in her position might have been looking ahead to retirement, Brookner set off on a new career and took ten years off her age. When a friend pointed out the discrepancy in the dates, Brookner wrote with aplomb to *The Times* in London, "I am 47, and have been for ten years."[10] Such responses bring the comedy of London music halls to mind, but Brookner's first novel harkens back more to the household on Herne Hill, the well-off London suburb where she grew up. Like herself, her protagonist would be an only child whose intelligence provides no safety net from future disappointments. Schooling as a poor preparation for succeeding in the real world, which is so forcefully introduced in this novel, would continue to be a recurring theme in her next eighteen novels.

If Brookner's vision of the world seems harsh, her experience of academic achievement and private disillusionment might provide some reasons why. Having excelled at James Allen's Girls School in Dulwich and King's College, London, where she received a degree in history, Brookner went on to the prestigious Courtauld Institute of Art in London. There she completed a doctorate in art history and came under the wing of its director, Anthony Blunt, who played an important part in encouraging her in her work. In perhaps Britain's most notorious spy case, Blunt, who had been among other things curator for Buckingham Palace, was found to have been working for the KGB along with Kim Philby, Guy Burgess, and Donald MacLean.

It was not until Peter Wright's book *Spycatcher* came out in 1987 that Brookner learned she had been a pawn in Blunt's spying operations. In "A Stooge of the Spycatcher," printed in the British journal *The Spectator* in that same year, Brookner claims her innocence in the whole affair. If Brookner is to be believed, the impact of these revelations must have been considerable. This is not merely because of the notoriety of the case but also because of the significance she has attached to her male mentors, her grandfather and father, before Blunt. The ironies must have been inescapable, not the least of them being the correlation now between art and secrets, friendship and betrayal.

Whether paintings in the National Gallery in London or the photographs in a family album, pictures are treated as private sources of knowledge by Brookner's protagonists. In *The Misalliance* (1986), for example, Blanche Vernon bases her view of an unjust world on the images of nymphs who, like certain women, are engaging though selfish and idle. *Family and Friends* (1985) has as its premise the imaginative construction of a family chronicle from two wedding portraits. *Incidents in the Rue Laugier* (1995) is a similar piecing together of things that, like the cryptic notebook of the protagonist's enigmatic mother, resemble the paraphernalia associated with espionage and spy fiction.

Assembling materials accurately is, however, not always the forte of Brookner's protagonists. This is especially true of those— ranging from Kitty Maule in *Providence* (1982) to Claire Pitt in *Undue Influence* (1999)—whose counterparts are male. Coded messages and signals are their lot to crack in the pursuit, often to the bitter end, of the truth they seek. Am I desired? is the question they most want to ask. With lovers unforthcoming, answers are hard to come by. Too often, what is a game for others is something considerably more serious for these protagonists. When they find themselves abandoned through no fault of their own, the tragedy is complete.

At thirty-nine Brookner was appointed Slade Professor of Art at the University of Cambridge for the 1967–68 year. What would have been honor enough for any scholar, let alone one who considers herself outside the English establishment, was heightened by the fact that no woman before Brookner had ever been granted such an honor. Afterward, she was made a fellow of New Hall, Cambridge, and a Fellow of King's College, and received honorary doctorates from the University of Loughborough in Britain and Smith College in the United States. In 1990, Brookner was made a Commander of the British Empire.

It is with her writing career that Brookner's personal life has come most under scrutiny. Given the preponderance of female protagonists in her novels, this can hardly be surprising. The risk is that the autobiographical tag can be too readily applied to novels based on little more than the gender and single status of a protagonist, thereby devaluing the creative integrity of the writer. Then, when a novel such as *Latecomers* (1988) comes along, it seems to mark more changes than continuity in Brookner's work. An overemphasis on protagonists' gender and marital status can divert attention from the development of themes of displacement and exile that have featured since *The Debut*. The fact that a male protagonist does not feature until *Latecomers* has led many critics to equate her novels strictly with novels about lonely women. Even a catalog from Penguin published in 2000 refers to her work as "Brookner's 'spinster' novels." Nonetheless, British sales alone of the Booker Prize winner *Hotel du Lac,* which would subsequently be made in to a highly acclaimed BBC film starring Anna Massey and Denholm Elliott, were nothing short of phenomenal. Within two weeks of publication on September 6, 1984, it had sold out. By January of 1985, over fifty-one thousand copies had been sold in Britain, nearly twenty times the number her first novel had sold.[11]

Since 1981 Brookner's readers have come to expect, without fail, that a new novel will appear each year. This annual output, which began during her summers free from teaching, has inadvertently fueled some criticism. Because of her prolific production, Brookner's novels tend to meet with reviews that contain the words "yet again" or "yet another." The similarity of themes, even the similar London setting and class background of her characters, can also contribute to the view that Brookner is less artist than recycler. Another factor working against her at times has been her remarks in interviews. Taking it as an absolute when Brookner told Shusha Guppy in a 1987 interview for the *Paris Review* that she *never* rewrites, Joyce Carol Oates insinuates a lack of professionalism because Brookner has no "writerly interest in revision."[12]

If the literary community is divided when it comes to Brookner, admirers nonetheless outnumber detractors. Among the latter, however, hostility can run high. Peter Kemp, a reviewer for the British *Sunday Times,* wanted to "stamp out" Brookner's *Lewis Percy* (1989), the first of her novels to feature a single male protagonist.[13] Elsewhere, inaccuracies in some reviews raise the question how far beyond the title page some critics have read. Angela McRobbie, a reviewer for the British journal the *New Statesman,* claims, for example, that the protagonist of *Hotel du Lac* "is recovering from an adulterous affair by taking a holiday."[14] Edith Hope has every intention of remaining the mistress of the man she loves. This much is obvious when she calls him to her bed only hours after she leaves another man standing at the altar. Those who read Brookner's novels to the end more often than not praise her portraiture of disappointed lives. In France, Brookner's has been called incomparable for her mastery of *minutie cruelle,* cruel detail.[15] And in Britain and the United States, comparisons have been made to Jane Austen and Henry James.

In spite of interviews in which Brookner makes no secret of her Jewish upbringing and regrets that she missed out on Hebrew lessons because her parents thought her health too delicate for her to withstand such demands, her writing exhibits few of the features commonly associated with Jewish writing. The absence of characters clearly designated as Jewish and omission of the word Jew entirely from novels in which they do feature have led some critics to accuse her of a "self-conscious refusal to engage with this [Jewish] culture."[16] Others strictly regard Brookner's writing as English. The publication in 1988 of *Latecomers,* however, calls for a reassessment of Brookner's writing and its place in Jewish literature.

Although the Holocaust provides the backdrop to other novels such as *Family and Friends* (1985) and *Dolly* (1993), in *Latecomers* it is center stage. As a result, any discussion of the traditions in which Brookner is working must thereafter include those of Holocaust writing. Reflecting on the contributions made in this area, Elie Wiesel is not alone in seeing the problematics of dealing with a subject of such magnitude. His advice, particularly to nonsurvivor novelists who treat the Holocaust, is to learn "the art of economy and what the French call *pudeur* (modesty)."[17] At best, they might develop the skill to condense situations and themes "to the point at which they burst from within" thereby conveying the emotional and mental devastation that lies concealed.[18] None of Brookner's characters directly witnesses the Holocaust. Yet the two male protagonists of *Latecomers* bear its legacies long after they are sent on a children's transport train to England from Germany, never to see their families again. Brookner's natural economy and aversion to excesses of language and dramatizing, which had been honed with each consecutive novel, seemed to be building to this moment. Meeting her subject head on, Brookner avoids the pitfalls of writers who trivialize the Holocaust by making it "no more than a heuristic device for maintaining ethnic identity."[19] And in spite of her customary lack of

engagement with Jewish culture, she does not shy away from showing the Jewish specificity of the Holocaust. In confronting the problem, How is it possible to live after destruction? *Latecomers* can be
viewed as "contemporary midrash to an ancient Jewish question."[20]

The task of *keeping* Brookner within any one tradition, however, would take effort. For all the similarity of themes and style, her
novels evade easy classification. Even the label of Jewish writer
poses difficulties. Grouping her with Emanuel Litvinoff has its purpose in an anthology aimed at introducing readers to the existence
of Anglo-Jewish writing. But like the *inteligencja* Jew who tells
the former *shtetl* dweller, "Your Warsaw is not my Warsaw,"
Brookner's London is not an East Ender's London.[21] Brookner was
born into a well-off family of Continental European entrepreneurs,
one that went on to have its own factory in Britain. As a child she
had a nanny, and there were servants in her home.

Where memoirists such as Litvinoff recall the material poverty
of a Jewish immigrant community, Brookner writes about emotional
need among well-off second- and third-generation non-English and
the English themselves alike. Instead of setting out to re-create a his-
torically specific time and place, Brookner's aims are largely divorced
from Jewish or even British history. This is evident even from her
settings. Interiors dominate over any number of street scenes, which
are generally deserted by all but her protagonists when they do ven-
ture out. The homebound settings draw the reader's attention literally in rather than out, thereby reflecting Brookner's focus on the
inner workings of her protagonists' minds. Given this focus, there is
little in the way of local color, ethnic or otherwise, in her novels. The
absence of any but the most implicit historical markers is comparable

to her avoidance of overwriting or commercial pressures to include gratuitous sex.

Looking even briefly at her work in Britain as an art critic for the *Times Literary Supplement* and book reviewer for the *Spectator* reveals not only Brookner's artistic and literary tastes but her aims as a novelist as well. The two defining features of her novels might be said to be language that informs without embellishment or dramatization and a form that barely ever calls attention to itself. With the first, Brookner is adamant: Less is more. Repetition, if uncontrolled, "negates the effect of the whole." Saying something once, in fact, can make it "all the more significant" in a text.[22] Writing that is concise earns her praises. Yet even these features are simply and plainly expressed ("The brevity with which the information is disclosed is admirable").[23]

Beyond succinctness, there is the matter of omission. Sex is a prime example of this characteristic of Brookner's fiction. Brookner's characters may have it, even a fair amount of it, but her novels are generally devoid of what are conventionally considered to be sex scenes. Dismissing what she calls "obligatory torrid episodes," Brookner promotes instead the benefit of descriptions of daily routine or "those small-town details."[24] The keyword here is "obligatory." In fiction, as in the lives of her protagonists, sex that is de rigeur might as well not happen at all. Unless sufficient impetus comes from within a text, sex scenes will be mere filler. It is important to distinguish between the veritable absence of sex scenes in Brookner's novels and her protagonists' libidinous tastes. Their ideal of exalted physicality is most readily captured in an ordinary moment transformed by extraordinary feelings such as the touch of an arm. "Sensual chastity," or "chaste sensuality," as Brookner calls it, may seem to harken back to times far removed from the present, but its power on the page remains unmatched.[25]

In *Hotel du Lac,* the romance writer Edith Hope defends her books by saying "those multi-orgasmic girls with the executive briefcases can go elsewhere. They will be adequately cared for. There are hucksters in every market place."[26] Brookner's novels are devoid of the conventions such as a formulaic happy ending, and their author stands as firm as Edith Hope when it comes to her refusal to bow to popular tastes. The great number of her novels with unhappy if not shocking endings, particularly in the early 1980s— for example, *The Debut, Providence, Look at Me,* and more recently, *Undue Influence,* published in 1999—could lead to the conclusion that she also rejects optimism. Yet the existence of novels such as *Hotel du Lac, The Misalliance,* and *Latecomers* with more ambiguous if not exactly happy endings indicates otherwise.

In interviews, Brookner has a way of speaking about her novels' characters that makes them seem independent of her pen, as if their fates were their own, not her, doing. She distances herself from a writer like Flaubert who "*wants* his characters to be defeated," suggesting instead that her characters are destined to their fates because of their personalities and dispositions.[27] Taking the position that events should at least appear to come about if not inevitably, then naturally, she believes that nothing the writer does should seem forced.

All of Brookner's nineteen novels share a similarity in form that can be summed up as follows. Each is short. Just either side of two hundred pages is the norm. A close-up rather than a wide-angle lens is employed to focus on a single protagonist or relationship, often within a brief time span. External factors such as historical and political events remain outside the scope of all novels but those in which the Holocaust is an integral part.

Plots are simple to the point of barely existing. Action is minimal. So is dialogue. Narration is uppermost in importance, particularly as it allows entreé into the unarticulated thoughts and emotions of characters. Since reticence is the quality that typifies protagonists and the English generally, as opposed to the Irish and continental Europeans in her novels, reliance on narrators is considerable. This is not to say that all are equally trustworthy. *Incidents in the Rue Laugier* raises some doubts in that area. But this is an exception to the rule. Overall, whether they are first-person protagonist/narrators or third-person omniscient ones, they all clearly fulfill the purpose of relating the story at hand without the divagations that many postmodern writers would allow them.

In a review of an exhibit of the eighteenth-century French painter François Boucher's work in Paris, Brookner speaks of the "contract" between painter and spectator.[28] She uses the same term when warning of the pitfalls of the postmodern novel ("the writer's contract with the reader has been arbitrarily renegotiated . . . [the result] is too often incoherent").[29] Coherence in Boucher's painting, according to Brookner, comes from his control and handling, which keep the subject from being depleted and allow the technique alone to be admired. Similarly, Brookner's writing can be said to serve her subjects well, never depleting them for all that its elegance draws praise. In words that would serve as a fine retort to criticism that her writing is formulaic because her novels are nearly all the same length and treat similar themes, Brookner claims that the term formulaic more accurately describes the product of current literary fashions. For instance, when John Updike "goes post-modern" there is a loss of his former "captivating fluency."[30] Such observations might especially serve as a warning to lesser writers. As for readers, the implication of Brookner's comments is "Buyer beware."

The writers whom Brookner admires are those with whom she has the most obvious affinity in background and interests. Among them are many women writers particularly "of foreign extraction who write in a totally different tradition [from the English]: Edith Templeton, a Czech who writes in impeccable English . . . [about] old-style central Europe, with recognizable passions and follies"; "Mavis Gallant, a Canadian writer living in Paris . . . working on the Dreyfus case"; and Edith de Born from Belgium who, according to Brookner, exhibits none of the sentimentality of English writers.[31] Even in this small grouping a pattern emerges that is useful toward understanding Brookner's writing. To begin with, attention to language is foremost. It should be nothing short of flawless. Second, the setting need not be exclusively English or for that matter the former British Empire. Central Europe has a richness of material. So too does Jewish history. It does not take much imagination to understand Brookner's interest in the infamous Dreyfus case of the 1890s, in which a Jewish officer, Captain Alfred Dreyfus, was wrongly accused by the French of spying for the Germans. Besides epitomizing anti-Semitism and the precariousness of assimilation, it has become virtually synonymous with injustice—the single most important theme of her novels. Finally, there is an indication of the desired tone of the telling, which in Brookner's writing never lapses into sentimentality.

In addition to the women writers whom Brookner admires, the men who impress her also serve as a window onto her own work.

Lamenting "the short attention span of readers and critics" who failed to appreciate Kazuo Ishiguro's *The Unconsoled,* Brookner argues that an absence of action can actually lend drama to a text. Delays, especially when repeated, can be "the stuff of nightmare," that which makes a situation Kafkaesque.[32] For Brookner's protagonists, like Ishiguro's concert pianist Ryder, this comes frequently in the form of waiting in hotel rooms. What does *not* happen underscores what does, thereby making momentous even the most seemingly unmomentous scene. Thus in *Family and Friends* (1985) Mimi learns the hard way that inviting a man to your bed does not necessarily mean he will appear. The loss of innocence that Mimi experiences as she waits for a sexual encounter that never occurs is no less powerful an awakening for its lack of event. First, the entire fate of this character is determined by this incident. Second, the fate is unjust.

Like Jean Rhys, whom she admires, Brookner chooses a subject who is an underdog. Although her women are not financially dependent on men as are Rhys's, they are irrevocably reliant on them in other ways. This theme receives particular attention in the first four novels featuring single female protagonists. *The Debut, Providence, Look at Me,* and *Hotel du Lac* all have love as their focus. Read in sequence, the effect is similar to the trilogy formed by Rhys's *Voyage in the Dark* (1934), *After Leaving Mr. Mackenzie* (1930), and *Good Morning, Midnight* (1939). With each novel, the female protagonist advances in age and knowledge after undergoing trials of courtship in which marriage never materializes. Rather than merely relating tales of romantic failure, Brookner, like Rhys, is depicting a world in which the oppressed are undeserving of their fate.

Since men come to embody much of the hypocrisy and cruelty that their protagonists suffer, *The Debut, Providence, Look at Me,* and *Hotel du Lac* might seem to be indictments of gender oppression. Yet the presence of female nemeses, who are spared the same mistreatment but who then mistreat Brookner's protagonists, counters such a reading. Another reason to conclude that these novels are concerned with more than gender relations is the juxtaposition of foreign, or outsider, female protagonists with English, or insider, male romantic interests. In this regard, a postcolonial reading (one that stresses the complexities of the condition of the ethnic outsider within former colonial cultures) of these texts is not out of place. If the complexities of Brookner's first novels have escaped the attention of many critics, this may have as much to do with common assumptions about woman writers as with the subject of love itself.

A departure from the focus on single female protagonists and rites of courtship occurs with the publication in 1985 of Brookner's *Family and Friends.* As with previous treatments of intimate lives, this family chronicle has a wider scope than may at first be apparent. While the trials with love are all there, so too is the Holocaust. Although it does not undermine this German Jewish family's existence in England, it links its members to a history and suffering beyond itself and the shores of their adopted home. The annihilation of Jews in Europe also lends a poignancy to the otherwise unexceptional events in the lives of this immigrant family. Children are inherently significant in any family chronicle. The backdrop of the Holocaust and the fact that this family is Jewish serve to elevate children and the whole notion of generation and continuance to a symbolic level.

UNDERSTANDING ANITA BROOKNER

Children continue to be the focus in Brookner's next three novels. In *The Misalliance* (1986) and *A Friend from England* (1987), single female protagonists seek belonging with other people's families. This is not the first time that orphans have featured in Brookner's novels. Here, however, they do not look to a male love interest, but to a child, to change their lives. In *The Misalliance,* a childless middle-aged woman whose husband has left her for a younger woman tries to earn the affection of a mute toddler and her frivolous young mother. Each has been displaced from a marriage, home, or place in society, yet an alliance proves to be as doomed as it is unnatural. *A Friend from England* similarly depicts a protagonist's ill-fated longing for acceptance into a family not her own.

With *Latecomers* (1988), Brookner returns to the subject of the Holocaust in a highly psychological and moving depiction of two aging Englishmen whose beginnings as child refugees from Germany color the remainder of their lives. Freudian psychoanalysis provides a virtual subtext for this novel, in which one of its protagonists pursues the childhood that his memory has repressed. In this, as in *The Misalliance* and *A Friend from England,* feelings of displacement motivate protagonists to find belonging in families. The irony perhaps is that *Family and Friends,* which introduced this theme, depicts a family that starts off intact. Yet the threat or reality of displacement is never far beneath the surface. Even the family business (transplanted from Europe like the one in Brookner's own family) is a reminder that England is only an adopted home. There is no question that Sofka's children are her own. But their connection to England is tenuous to say the least, as the immigration of Betty to the United States and Frederick to Italy illustrates.

Brookner turns from children to the subject of marriage most fully in her next three novels: *Lewis Percy* (1989), *Brief Lives* (1990), and *A Closed Eye* (1991). Following her depiction of the pursuit and idealization of marriage in her first four novels, Brookner presents its disappointing reality. Although male, the protagonist of *Lewis Percy* is the archetypal Brookner protagonist in holding romantic ideals. For him, as for the female protagonists of *Brief Lives* and *A Closed Eye,* a marriage lacking in passion is not merely an entrapment but can be likened to a form of death. Yet it is not freedom alone that is sought after; rather it is the life-affirming energy that comes with desire. Adultery is thus depicted as something highly complex and beyond mere sex or even love. Although a form of betrayal, it is presented as a lesser deception than upholding the guise of a happy marriage.

Transformations are much sought after by Brookner's protagonists, from the wishful Kitty in *Providence* and depressive Fibich in *Latecomers* to the physically and emotionally scarred Harriet in *A Closed Eye*. Whether its attainment is envisaged through love, family, marriage, or an elicit affair, it is dependent on another person. The alternative is that Brookner's protagonists come to resemble the figure of the wandering Jew if left on their own for too long. Their minds like their bodies are rarely at ease. Lengthy passages of introspection and scenes in which they walk with no clear destination help to evoke parallels to the wandering Jew who deserves no such fate.

Whereas death is no release for ghosts, it provides the chance for flesh-and-blood protagonists to start again in *Fraud* (1992), *Dolly* (1993), and *A Private View* (1994). Since second chances are rarely handed out to Brookner's protagonists, whose fates are usually determined with a single event (or nonevent, as is the case with Mimi in *Family and Friends*), these novels exhibit an optimism that belies their somber beginnings. One reason for this is the resilience their protagonists show despite of all their hardships. These protagonists are considerably older than those in Brookner's earlier novels, yet they are not jaded by their experiences, which makes them surprisingly inspiring. Of them all, the aunt in *Dolly* is the most memorable. She is first seen through the eyes a child, an unusual twist in a Brookner novel and one that works perfectly to foreshadow a magnificence of character that is only first perceived as physical immensity. The contrast between an old-world Jewish set of beliefs and the status quo is also a feature of *Dolly*. Humor and hope may have come late to Brookner's writing but are worth waiting for with this novel.

Incidents in the Rue Laugier (1995), *Altered States* (1996), and *Visitors* (1997) have in common the depiction of a journey. While it is generally true that Brookner's protagonists go on them almost as much as they think of them, in these novels mental journeys take priority. The reverse might seem to be the case with *Incidents in the Rue Laugier,* in which characters crisscross France and England. But the entire story of Maude Gonthier is in reality just a mental exercise, a construct of the daughter/narrator's imagination. The fact that the mother around whom this narrative is constructed is dead is highly significant. For in the narrative she is effectively brought back to life. In the absence of a greater "creator" in the worlds of Brookner's novels, the writer-as-creator analogy has special meaning. It is found again in *Altered States,* where a male protagonist's only good act in life is when he tells stories to an elderly Polish relation. In this, as in *Visitors,* the ultimate journey which awaits these characters of advancing years is death. How they travel to this end with dignity is very much the subject of these novels.

Brookner's last two novels of the 1990s feature a return to the themes and style of earlier novels. Both have single female protagonists whose unmarried state is likened to a form of exile. Desire for belonging and a sense of home are conveyed in such a way that protagonists in such a predicament epitomize the outsider. As with Brookner's first four novels, which treat this theme, single women are figures of displacement in society. Friendships between women are few because they must compete with one another to alter their situation. In *Falling Slowly* (1998) this reality lends tension to the relationship between two sisters. In *Undue Influence* (1999), Brookner depicts a Darwinian order in which women who are not predators are doomed. Not since *Providence* has the focus been so much on a protagonist's yearning to attract a male object of desire. The failure of Claire Pitt to do so provides no less of a shocking end for this novel than in earlier ones.

Brookner creates characters who seem fated for easier lives. The fact that they are less deserving than Brookner's protagonists and are frequently depicted as representing English society makes the resulting image of England indeed a damning one. Tea and sympathy come in short measure. The cold shoulder, like the cold omelette, is standard fare. For Brookner's protagonists who are so regularly depicted as foundlings, England is a cruel stepmother.

Without exception, Brookner's novels chronicle her protagonists' realization that life is not what they expected it to be and, in her later novels particularly, how they maintain their dignity in spite of their disappointments. For this reason, the fascination that many readers have with her writing might seem to be a form of perversion—

a sadistic pleasure in witnessing the dashed hopes and dreams of yet another of her protagonists. Yet repulsion and a refusal to accept this view of the world underlie even admiring responses to her writing. As one critic puts it, "I have never before been addicted to a writer with whose values and vision I so consciously disagree."[33]

There is no denying that Brookner's nineteen novels present a bleak view of the world. Yet without exception her protagonists espouse a more positive view; their faith in a better world than this is their tragedy. It is also their beauty. The power of an ideal vision is implicit in each novel's message that the world is unjust. Perhaps even a "dark" aesthetic can be assimilated as an aesthetic. The beauty of Brookner's novels is not in the isolated message but in the telling.

CHAPTER TWO

Can't Buy Me Love
The Debut, Providence, Look at Me,
and *Hotel du Lac*

The Debut

I started writing because of a terrible feeling of powerlessness: I felt I was drifting and obscure, and I
rebelled against that.

Anita Brookner, interview with John Haffenden

Aspiring writers are conventionally told to get the first novel out of
the way so they can get on to better things. Anita Brookner's *The
Debut* (1981) is a first novel that discredits such advice. Its excel-
lence was noted from the start by critics who praised it as a "precise
and haunting little performance" and its author for her "impeccable
prose and sly wit" as well as "precision and perception and confidence of the telling."[1] While Brookner admits that *The Debut* is an
autobiographical first novel, it suffers none of the drawbacks commonly associated with the type.[2] Reflecting a desire for control in
her personal life, Brookner's style is characteristically one of control
over her material, however intimate it may be. For example, the likeness between Ruth's parents in *The Debut* and Brookner's own is
striking. Although expressing her love for them, she says, "They
should have never had children; they didn't understand children and
couldn't be bothered."[3] The words are Brookner's, but anyone could
be forgiven for thinking they were Ruth's from *The Debut*. The message is the same. Some people make terrible parents, but their children can be devoted to them anyway. Saying that her parents "were
just as bizarre but not quite so fetching" as those she creates for *The*

CAN'T BUY ME LOVE

Debut, Brookner reveals the essential difference separating the unskilled from the skilled novelist.[4] Whereas the former is virtually controlled by the subject matter, the latter is prepared to "improve" on reality to write a good novel.

The Debut, Providence, Look at Me, and *Hotel du Lac* loosely function as a cycle. The similarities between protagonists and their gradually advancing years contribute to this view. So too does the pursuit of love, acceptance, even rescue as a recurring theme. Just as this first novel marks both beginnings and endings in Brookner's professional life, spelling the end of her career as an art critic as she turns to the writing of fiction, *The Debut* (or *A Start in Life* as it is known in Britain) is as much about endings as beginnings for its protagonist. Brookner introduces this theme with the opening words of the novel: "Dr. Ruth Weiss, at forty, knew that her life had been ruined by literature . . . when, at a faintly remembered moment in her early childhood, she had fallen asleep, enraptured, as her nurse breathed the words 'Cinderella *shall* go to the ball.' But the ball had never materialized."[5] What unfolds in the chapters that follow is how a fairytale start does not guarantee a fairytale ending. Unlike Cinderella, Ruth Weiss is never rescued by a Prince Charming. Her virtue is exploited, not rewarded. Consequently, she perceives her life to have been "ruined by literature" because the moral order it upholds proves to have no bearing in reality.

The first pages of *The Debut* "give away" its unhappy ending long before it occurs by placing together the stories of Cinderella and Ruth Weiss in opposition to one another. While this might diminish the dramatic impact of events in *The Debut,* it serves to lend interest to an otherwise unexceptional protagonist by building anticipation of her demise. What comes to mind are the beginnings of Aesop's fables, Kipling's *Just So Stories* (1902), with titles such as "How the Camel Got His Hump," and other tales for children meant to provide moral instruction. But whereas fables traditionally show the reward of good behavior and the punishment of bad behavior, contemporary texts evoking this model do not always follow suit. Fates are not always justly handed out. *The Debut* similarly raises the question *how* is Ruth "ruined by literature" or more precisely *how* do certain moral ideals come to be viewed by her as "faulty" (7).

Brookner in no way suggests that Ruth deserves to be ruined, or that this was ever the intention of her parents and nurse who guided her reading. The words "faulty moral education" imply that an error in judgment was made, one that is no less damaging for its lack of ill intent (7). The tone of *The Debut* is reflective, understated, and never vindictive. Yet from the start of the novel, the importance of childhood and the role that parents play in determining one's future is implicit in every word, even when Ruth only indirectly blames her parents by placing the blame on the literature they handed to her.

The importance of literature to Brookner's protagonists is a common feature and never more so than in her first four novels: *The Debut* (1981), *Providence* (1982), *Look at Me* (1984), and *Hotel du Lac* (1985). These four rely heavily on intertextual elements to produce parallels between the fate of Brookner's protagonists and the fate of protagonists in the books in their possession. The virtual model for them all is Ruth, the protagonist of *The Debut,* who is a university teacher writing a multivolume study called *Women in Balzac's Novels* (8). Ruth is currently working on Balzac's *Eugénie Grandet,* a story of "hopeless love." Her interest in Balzac began at university when she wrote her dissertation on "Vice and Virtue in

Balzac's Novels" (9, 36). Given Ruth's consistently virtuous behavior, her choice of subject is an ironic one foreshadowing other ironies to come in her life because "Balzac teaches the supreme effectiveness of bad behaviour" (36). The validity of such a vision is something that Ruth as a young student was only "beginning to perceive" (36).

By the time Ruth is forty, her age at the start of the novel, she will conclude that it would have been better as a child to have read Balzac than Hans Christian Andersen, the Brothers Grimm, and Dickens, who taught that "virtue would surely triumph, [and] patience would surely be rewarded" (11). Had her nurse read her a translation of *Eugénie Grandet,* she would have learned that what matters is not "moral fortitude" (9). Happiness comes to those who are "engaging" and "attractive" (9). This message is encapsulated in two extracts from Balzac that conclude the first subsection of chapter 1: "Je ne suis pas assez belle pour lui" and "'Aussi,' se dit-elle en se mirant, sans savoir encore ce qu'était l'amour: 'Je suis trop laide, il ne fera pas attention à moi'" (I am not pretty enough for him *and* "Also," she said looking at herself, without knowing what love was: "I am too ugly, he won't pay any attention to me") (9). Brookner's interspersing of French phrases at this point underlines the significance of these truths for the protagonist in two ways. First, the French stands out from the rest of the English text just as its message stands in opposition to everything that Ruth had been taught from childhood. Second, the absence of a translation (which Brookner does provide for the French passages in *Providence*) lends an air of secrecy to words that Ruth later regards as a revelation. Elsewhere, the interspersing of French phrases is employed ironically. The teenaged Ruth's zeal in learning French is epitomized by her love of reciting passages aloud to herself in her bedroom. Her cries of "Pars courageusement" (Go with courage) and "laisse toutes les villes!" (leave all the towns!) seem at first to have no significance beyond the fact that they are foreign words for Ruth (23). Yet their message, had she understood at the time, might have altered the course of her life altogether. For it is Ruth's sense of filial duty that destines her to a lonely middle age, one that might never have been her fate if she had had the courage to leave London and her duties behind.

Another example of how Brookner supplies seemingly inconsequential details while at the same time omitting significant pieces of information is her use of misleading information. After writing that the protagonist of *The Debut* teaches literature at a university, this unexceptional fact is lent interest by the following postulations: "Murderers, great criminals, should ideally be dons; plenty of time to plan the coup and no curious questions or inquisitive glances once it is done. Dr. Weiss's colleagues maintained a state of perfect indifference to her past life. . . . Dr. Weiss's pale face prompted no speculation whatsoever" (10). Murderers and "great criminals" are not found in Brookner's writing. Death is a regular feature, but predominantly from natural causes such as cancer or heart failure and frequently following long periods of invalidism. Violent deaths do not occur, with the exception of car accidents in *The Debut* and *A Closed Eye,* car and plane crashes in *Falling Slowly,* and a suicide in *Visitors,* all of which are related without sensationalizing and with the barest minimum of words. "Great criminals" are also absent, although con artists figure prominently with devastating or comic effect in *The Misalliance, A Friend from England, Fraud,* and *A Private View.*

Like *Providence, Look at Me,* and the McConnell Booker Prize winner *Hotel du Lac, The Debut* is about love. It features a single female protagonist who is primarily shown from young childhood to the age of twenty-two when the remainder of her life is determined for her. Like the protagonists of these novels, Ruth Weiss is intelligent, educated, and financially independent. Like the traditionally perceived image of Cinderella, she is also impoverished. Starved for affection since childhood, Ruth perceives happiness in terms of male love that would rescue her from loneliness as well as from servitude to her family.

Perhaps as a preparation for difficult adult lives, difficult childhoods are a common feature of Brookner's novels. *The Debut* is no exception. Chapter 2 begins with the protagonist's memory of herself as a child who is rushed into adulthood by her nurse, who "had been patient but brisk" and had expected her "to grow up as fast as she could decently manage it, and to this end was supplied with sad but improving books" (11). Nature as well seems to be rushing her maturity. The "extraordinary hair that made her head ache" seems more suitable for an adult than a child (11). Its volume and weight reflect the burdensomeness of even the simplest tasks. Even replacing a cup into its saucer caused Ruth "a great effort," as evidenced by her "tongue protruding gracelessly" when she tried to put it in "the exact depression" (11). In this single image, Brookner depicts a world in which correct behavior is presented as the ideal and one that is frequently painful to exact.

If childhood is thought of as play, school, and time spent with other children, Ruth seems to have hardly had a childhood. Isolation rather than socialization characterizes the years preceding adulthood, thereby making her a figure of loneliness from the start. Brookner conveys this view as much by omission as any information the omnipresent narrator supplies. The major omission is of any scenes in classrooms, schoolyards, or any other settings where the protagonist could be seen alongside other children. In only one scene is the protagonist at school at all. This is when she is about to leave and is in an office with her teacher and parents. Adults surround the protagonist in every instance. As a result, although she is not alone, she is an isolated figure who is set apart from others. The absence of any scenes in settings where one might conventionally expect to find children is particularly significant because it compounds the sense of Ruth's isolation within her own home. Typical of Brookner's protagonists, Ruth is an only child. Because she is outnumbered by adults, her place in the home is virtually that of an outsider. For the center of attention in this home is never the protagonist of *The Debut,* any more than it is the protagonists in any of Brookner's other novels. As a microcosm for the adult world that lies ahead, the childhood home is a place in which the protagonist only peripherally belongs and matters significantly less than its other members.

Yet Ruth is not marginalized because of her lack of family status. Hers is a household not of stepsisters and a stepmother but her own parents, paternal grandmother, nurse, and maid. In this regard, her marginalization seems even crueler than Cinderella's, because it lacks any basis at all for justification. Perhaps the single most distinguishing feature of Brookner's novels is the way events befall their protagonists instead of being perpetrated by them. The pattern, which is set from childhood, is of a protagonist's responding to and trying to make sense of the actions of others, actions that are too often inexplicably cruel.

The nature of Ruth's deprivation at home can be understood from looking at those instances when she is barely happy. Words for *happiness* are so rarely associated with Brookner's protagonists (as opposed to the undeserving and selfish people around her) that any break in this pattern cannot go without notice. In chapter 16 of *The Debut,* Brookner does just this, not once, but twice in quick succession. The first instance concerns the protagonist's thoughts. "It would soon be her turn to be happy," Ruth thinks after hearing of the marriage of a man she had once wanted for herself and of news of the impending birth of a child to the English couple who out of boredom had previously "adopted" her as a form of amusement (148). The second instance concerns her manner and voice. When her lover, Professor Duplessis, hears that she will soon have her own apartment, he says, "Perhaps you will make me a cake" (149). Her response is uncommonly resolute and provocative for a Brookner protagonist. "More," she confirmed happily (149).

What has prompted this change in spirit is the prospect of a change of address. She has already left London for Paris, but the maid's room that her mother arranges for her to take in the home of friends is virtually an extension of her childhood home and her peripheral status there. Getting her own apartment will mark the point of departure and entry into adulthood that leaving England did not. Her own needs can now be tantamount.

Professor Duplessis figures largely in her plans. But he does not fit the conventional picture of a prince charming. He is old enough to be her father and even has daughters the same age as the protagonist. Above all, he has a wife. There is never any suggestion that he will turn Ruth Weiss into Ruth Duplessis. Even in her most optimistic moments, the protagonist dreams not of marriage but of the physical consummation of their affair, which has had to be relegated to clandestine meetings in public places all winter. When she promises to give Professor Duplessis more than a home-baked cake, she is offering herself as more than a congenial hostess. This is evident from her thoughts, which range from her acceptance that he will not be able to spend the whole night (he will have "to leave her to go home") and the prospect of going away together to anticipated relief from the winter's "longer evenings [which] are frustrating" (148). If there remain any doubts as to the form of this frustration and the "sheer discomfort" that wants relief, Brookner alleviates these with Professor Duplessis's thoughts. From the first, there is no question that physical consummation of their affair is on both their minds. "He, an old married man," Brookner writes, "would soon be doing what everyone else already suspected him of doing. . . . His elegant wife would sit innocently in the rue de la Pompe" (149). The lack of sex scenes does not mean that Brookner is not writing about sex. The words "happy" and "happily" as applied to the protagonist point to a significance beyond the ordinary meanings of the words "cake" and "more" in this exceedingly brief but no less important piece of dia-logue.

A feminist reading of this passage might well focus on the tra-ditional associations of women with domestic duties that baking epitomizes. Ruth Weiss's "more" could be construed as the protago-nist's upholding of outdated models of womanhood and general subservience to men. In this case, her delight could not be viewed as anything less than inane. Brookner's protagonists would be better off learning how to eat and live happily on their own.[6] Consider instead that Ruth comes from a home in which she was emotionally *and* physically underfed. One of the first pleasures she foresees in having her own apartment is the freedom to "cook her own meals"

(148). The implication is that her days of mere subsistence living (both physically and emotionally) would end. The quick snack would give way to the abundance of a full-course dinner. Significantly, Professor Duplessis expresses his affection for her by asking if she eats well, by taking her out to dine, and by telling her (when she asks what she can give him) that she "must [first] learn to take" (115–16). Rather than being a naive acceptance of a model of women's servitude, Ruth's willingness to bake for her lover is steeped in self-interest. Having learned "to take" she could now give, and in so doing rise from the position of child to Professor Duplessis (who "had become both mother and father to her") to that of an adult on equal terms (149). Physical intimacy would finally spell the end to her daughter role as it heralded the start of her sexual maturity. Thus the position of mistress is perceived by the protagonist not to be degrading but empowering. She would have control. She would progress from being the neglected child of her parents and pampered child of Professor Duplessis to being an adult. At least this is what she expects to have happen.

In the circular patterning that is characteristic of Brookner's novels, Ruth is called back to London and her role as dutiful daughter at precisely that moment when she is about to embark on another route altogether. Two weeks after her promise of a cake and "more," she invites Professor Duplessis to her new apartment. This marks the first time in their relationship and her life that *she* has not been the one to wait. The power to determine the direction her life takes would seem to be in her hands. Yet her faith that the "omens were good" is continually countered by Professor Duplessis's unspoken feelings of foreboding (153).

In stark contrast to an earlier incident in the novel when a dinner for a young Englishman goes disastrously wrong, all indications are that the evening with Professor Duplessis is a culinary success.[7] But Ruth's ambitions go beyond being a good baker, which her desolation at the end of the evening confirms. This is because the cake serves as both a pretext for her meeting with Duplessis and as a symbol of their celebration of one another and the occasion of Ruth's new maturity or rebirth. What it launches in actuality, however, is no more a night of sexual union and the beginning of their future together than a new life for this protagonist. Yet this is not because she has misinterpreted their relationship. In England, she was wrong to have confused Richard Hirst's "acceptance of food with an offer of love."[8] In France, she reads the connection perfectly, making the evening with Duplessis very different from those scenes of sexual humiliation at dinner tables in *Providence* and *Look at Me*.[9] What happens is that Ruth is called back to London to care for her ailing parents. Eighteen years later she will still be carrying out these duties.

The way *The Debut* begins and ends with its protagonist at forty accentuates the circular patterning of events in the narrative. The affair with Professor Duplessis is reduced to an interlude without consequence insomuch as events of major consequence for Ruth are those perpetrated by others. Returning to London and the home of her parents, she is returned to the servitude that began from her childhood. While appearing to be a reversal of traditional roles for children and parents, assuming the role of caregiver is something that Ruth has had to do ever since childhood, when the death of her German-born grandmother left the household effectively without an adult head. With Ruth fated to a life of deferred pleasure as a consequence of being more able and mature than either of her parents,

The Debut introduces the theme that will feature time and again in Brookner's novels. Predestination will triumph over free will. People's lives are determined *for them* not *by them*. From birth, Ruth is fated to be both a daughter and an outsider within her own family. Like the hair that weighs down her head from childhood, this fate is a burden. Cutting her hair in Paris is thus equated with lightness or freedom and signifies the cutting of family ties in England.

While the burdens of being a daughter are quite obvious in *The Debut,* the reasons for Ruth's outsider status are less apparent. In this regard, Brookner offers clues rather than clear answers to explain this mystery surrounding the protagonist. For example, holidays that are traditionally associated with families getting together are in *The Debut* occasions when the protagonist is most alone (112). The illicit nature of the relationship with Professor Duplessis and a break from her London past are first suggested by the "forbidden" food that Ruth eats when they go out to dinner (116). Anti-Semitic remarks made by Ruth's mother start a series of cataclysmic events. From driving the father deeper into an affair to driving away the maid, these signal a breakdown in the parents' marriage and their daughter's plans for a future with Duplessis (124).

The sum of these and other details amounts to a more complex picture of the protagonist than at first appeared to be the case. This complexity arises from two major clashes in Ruth's background. The first of these is the clash between her mother's English background and her father's German one, presided over by her paternal grandmother, who emigrated to London from Berlin. The second is the clash between her mother's Catholicism and her father's Jewishness. Raised as neither Catholic nor Jewish, neither wholly English nor German, Ruth lacks connection to either parent and is effectively reduced to a foundling. Her lack of physical resemblance to either of them compounds this impression. She is also denied the means for identifying herself with other Jews or Catholics, ethnic Germans or the English. Paris offers a respite from such displacement, which in one's native country is an aberration but in a foreign country is to be expected and carries no shame. But whereas fairytale Cinderellas live *out of place* only until they move into castles, Brookner's protagonists seem fated to a life of exile in the absence of well wishing fairy godmothers.

Providence

> Quite simply, I lacked the information.
>
> *Providence,* 182

Brookner's protagonists are an unsettling bunch. Not exclusively female, young or old, single or married, they are frequently depicted as making those around them feel uncomfortable. Friendships are sporadic at best and, more often, trying relationships. The everyday seems weighed down with a self-consciousness and ritual that make the most ordinary social interactions of more than ordinary importance. When not unsettling those around them, Brookner's protagonists also have a tendency to go virtually unnoticed. They range from being an alien presence to a totally neutral one that barely seems to exist at all. Their ritualized lives, like Brookner's detailing of them, are mesmerizing in their orderliness, so that they come to be identified with order and things fitting neatly together. Yet at the same time, they do not fit easily anywhere.

Providence (1982) begins with the words "Kitty Maule was difficult to place." It ends with Kitty Maule's colleagues at a provincial English university once again trying to place her. "I must confess, Miss Maule, that we were discussing you before you arrived," says one professor. "We were trying to work out which half of you was French."[10] The circular narrative pattern of Brookner's *Providence* is emblematic of its protagonist's inability to fit in anywhere and resemblance on her habitual walks to the figure of a wandering Jew. Given that Kitty Maule's singular ambition is to attain a permanent place in society, what goes wrong? In order to answer this, one has to ask who she becomes in her pursuit of full acceptance into British society.

Providence begins and ends with its protagonist's explaining her background with the words "My father was in the army. He died before I was born" (5, 182). This is not a lie. But it is not the whole truth either, for Kitty Maule reinvents herself by omitting facts, in particular the facts of her mother's birth and background. Her mother's side, in the form of the grandparents who raise her, is regarded by Kitty Maule as a source of embarrassment and risk to her future, "for they were not like other people, and destined perhaps to designate the island of remoteness in Kitty's character which gave her so much trouble" (7). Describing the protagonist's virtual double life, Brookner begins with the sense of detail that one comes to expect, then goes off in another direction: "She had two homes; one, a small flat in Chelsea, where she kept her father's photograph, . . . the other, her grandparents' house in the suburbs, where, once inside the front door, one encountered the smells, the furnishings, the continual discussion that might take place in an apartment house in Paris or perhaps further east" (6). The words "perhaps further east" are not clarified until the next page, where it is revealed that Kitty Maule's grandfather, formerly a circus acrobat, is a Russian. The importance of the vague and almost euphemistic language used to describe this grandfather is central to the underlying tension in the entire narrative of *Providence*. While the protagonist would prefer to be accepted as thoroughly English, she does not wholly conceal her French background. Indeed, her colleagues ask which *half* of her is French, and she does nothing to correct the inaccuracy of this, preferring instead to obliterate any trace of her Russian ancestry. Considering the grandfather's role as father to the protagonist, his deep affection and way he is known as Papa to her, it is all the more significant that the protagonist chooses to conceal him altogether, in name, nationality, or presence. Instead, it is the biological English father (who dies before she is born) who is spoken of and whose framed portrait is the only family presence in Kitty Maule's Chelsea flat. The betrayal of one *father* for the other exemplifies the protagonist's calculating determination to achieve her aims. This stands in contrast to the seeming passivity that is characteristic of Brookner's protagonists. That she fails is another matter. More important, what can too easily be overlooked with regards to Kitty Maule as perhaps the quintessential Brookner female protagonist is her unbridled ambition: "I want more, she thought, blowing her nose resolutely. . . . I want to be totally unreasonable, totally unfair, very demanding, and very beautiful. I want to be part of a real family. I want my father to be there and to shoot things. . . . I want a future away from this place. I want Maurice" (59–60). The *wants* that Kitty Maule admits to are not for mere companionship or romantic love (she significantly never says she loves Maurice), but for the place in society that marriage to an upper-class Englishman would bring.

Though it can be argued that one cannot directly apprehend the existence of classes as "one can directly recognize the existence of women, of blacks, of the Catholic church, or of council housing estates," class exists for the characters in *Providence* because they, "explicitly or implicitly, recognize its existence and behave in ways which reflect its existence."[11] Kitty Maule is no exception. With the words "I want my father to be there and to shoot things," Brookner is expressing more than the wishful thinking of an orphan for a parent. The grandfather, Vadim, has, after all, served as a father figure and still does. Instead, the desire expressed is for *my* father, the English one, who is cast in the quintessential upper-class pastime of blood sports. Similarly, the words "I want a future away from this place. I want Maurice" are not so much the plaintive cry of a lonely woman as the sentiments of a pragmatist who sees that the only escape from a marginalized existence is to marry an insider. Background gives belonging. Failing that, one can only hope to marry someone with it. This is the reality of England that Kitty Maule and so many others face in Brookner's novels, a reality that differs considerably from the view that one's background, or the past, is something that, like "the old country," one can live without or leave behind.

What links Kitty Maule with the past is a male figure whose love and devotion is undeniable (like Lautner's for Sofka in *Family and Friends*), yet whose very presence is a reminder of her failure to be fully accepted as English. Like the "damp and overfilled" sandwiches that he presses on her and she later discards uneaten, Kitty Maule's grandfather is an unwanted presence. Yet unlike these reminders of him whose "smell hung disagreeably about her hands," hands she had to wash "several times" before handling her books on "the Romantic Tradition," grandfathers are harder to dispose of (15). Thus, "the transition from one life to another was not always easy" (15).

In *Providence,* as in all of Brookner's novels, family background is often an unendurable burden that runs contrary to the protagonists' aspirations for the future. If full assimilation is a means to attaining a new cultural identity, Kitty Maule's continued devotion to her grandparents is a definite obstacle in her way as she tries to balance two lives—weekdays in English academia, weekends in the home of her grandparents, where "one encountered the smells, the furnishings, the continual discussion that might take place in an apartment house in Paris or perhaps further east" (6).

As *The New Oxford Shorter English Dictionary* explains, "assimilation" is a form of "conversion" or "the action of making or becoming like." Inherent in these definitions is an understanding of assimilation as a process of conversion not only to but *from* something else and as an action of becoming *un*like a former self. For the protagonists in Brookner's novels this process specifically involves a rejection of blood relations or actual family for an adoptive family rooted in an alien culture. For Kitty Maule, this newfound family is the English academic community, and Maurice Bishop, like the favored son, is at its center. But as the circular pattern of downfall in this text suggests, "the transition from one life to another" is not only "not always easy" but, also, not always certain. *Providence* is essentially the story of an outsider who remains an outsider. What appears to be proved true is a theory of ancestral determinism over that of the individual, for Kitty Maule is never finally able to secure a future divorced from her parentage.

CAN'T BUY ME LOVE

Brookner's depiction of England in *Providence,* and to a greater and lesser extent in her other novels, is one in which the protagonist and all surrounding characters are virtually obsessed by background. Yet Kitty Maule does not perceive the future as beyond her control. Her failure to achieve full and lasting acceptance into English society is in no measure the result of lack of ambition, hard work, or drive. Kitty Maule uses such precise English that a blind woman remarks, "You rarely hear such good enunciation these days. It comes from her being a foreigner, of course. . . . The natives, after all, don't have to bother" (150).

This failure to *pass* for English foreshadows greater failures to come. Although she attains success in terms of career by the end of the novel, Kitty Maule fails to win Maurice Bishop. At a dinner in her honor, she finds herself reduced to someone who is neither lover, friend, nor least of all future wife. Significantly, her last words concern her identity. "My father was in the army," she says. "He died before I was born" (183). Once again the English father is given prominence over her mother, her Russian grandfather, or French grandmother, in a final attempt to secure her Englishness. But these words can do nothing to alter the fact that she is an outsider among insiders in this last scene. She alone does not know Maurice is going on to a post at Oxford. She alone offers to help Maurice in the kitchen, not knowing "the host" is already assisted by a "hostess," a former student of hers, at this dinner (182). "I lacked the information," she thinks. "Quite simply, I lacked the information" (182).

But a lack of information is not the problem for Kitty Maule. Difficulties in comprehending and arranging information are what bring about her downfall. Kitty Maule's efforts to stay composed, in spite of her shock during the dinner at Maurice's, proves she is a harsh realist *when* she can interpret the information she is given. Beforehand, however, like a foreigner to England (even an American speaker of English), she takes too literally the words "My love" and "Darling," which sprinkle Maurice Bishop's conversation (115). They are, she says, like "nourishment" to her, yet are meaningless to him (115).

A search for meaning that goes unsatisfied is introduced from the first chapter of *Providence*. Yet at this point in the novel, the questions are not those of Kitty Maule but her grandmother. The chapter concludes with an often-repeated scene of interrogation that may well explain why Kitty dreaded the weekends: "Well, *ma fille,* where are your lovers? Who will you take home tonight? For whom do you wash your hair? . . . I do not understand your life. Are your colleagues real men? Is it so different here? What do you discuss over your tea and biscuits? Come . . . come, *ma fille,* tell me about England" (16). But her grandmother's questions go unanswered with the opening chapter ending much as *Providence* does, with a protagonist who is regarded as "a marvelous foreigner" to her family yet who knows no more than they do about England (14). Typical of Brookner's protagonists, all of whom are displaced from birth or other circumstances, Kitty Maule is not only "difficult to place," she also has difficulty *finding* a place. Ultimately, Kitty Maule does not fully belong to either her grandparents' or Maurice's world.

Brookner's treatment of problems of identity and assimilation has been as largely ignored by critics as the fact of her Polish Jewish background, while her "Englishness" and similarity to Jane Austen are frequently cited. The exception is *Latecomers,* in which Brookner tells the story of the friendship between two Jewish men who come to England from Germany. The process of their assimilation follows that of their general maturity from boyhood to adulthood and has been read as such. *Latecomers,* however, is very much seen as less typically Brookner than her novels that have a single female protagonist. It would seem that those novels that focus on the loneliness of such a protagonist preclude any other concerns. But as *Providence* illustrates, the romantic interests of Brookner's protagonists can have wide-reaching social implications beyond love for another person.

Look at Me

> *Look at Me* is a very depressed and debilitated novel,
> and it's the one I regret. When I published it, a very
> old friend of my mother's summoned me and said,
> "You are getting yourself a bad reputation as a lonely
> woman. Stop it at once." She was right: it sticks.
> > Brookner, in interview with Haffenden

The cover of the British paperback edition of *Look at Me* is uncommonly disturbing for a Brookner novel. It features a detail from the painting "The Village of the Mermaids," by Paul Delvaux. In the distance, a group of mermaids enter the sea. In the foreground, others in long dresses sit as if awaiting gentlemen callers. Their vacant expressions, however, suggest none will show. Comparable to Delvaux's depiction of half-fish, half-human beings whose belonging is never complete either in the sea or on land, *Look at Me* concerns a figure whose lack of belonging seems irrevocably fated. But briefly at least, like the mermaids whose skirts cover their fins, Brookner's protagonist appears to have shed her outsider status.

Frances Hinton shares many of the qualities and features of Brookner's first two female protagonists. She is educated, well off, single, and a Londoner. Like Ruth Weiss and Kitty Maule, who teach literature at universities, Frances Hinton has more contact with books than people in her work as a librarian at a medical research institute. And like the protagonist to come in *Hotel du Lac,* she is also a writer. Given that Frances Hinton regards herself more as an observer than a participant in life and that she is largely shown in her place of work, where "silence is the rule," *Look at Me* is long on reflection and especially short on dialogue.[12] Being confined so much to its library setting and Frances Hinton's observations, this first person narrative moves exceedingly slowly, reflecting as it were the actual pace of this protagonist's life. Similarly, just as none of the library researchers' projects seems ever to be completed, her life appears to be one of fruitless routine.

From the first words of *Look at Me,* Brookner presents Frances Hinton as having no illusions about the world and the ability to look without blinking at painful and disturbing sights. Her profession demands this, as does her experience in life. The first sentences of the opening paragraphs tell us as much: "Once a thing is known it can never be unknown. It can only be forgotten. . . . My name is Frances Hinton and I do not like to be called Fanny" (5). In the ensuing pages, we are told in detail what horrific scenes are contained in the library archives. Yet the tone remains as matter-of-fact and impassive as at the start. What the archive images of incurable illness and mental torment foreshadow are the trials to come for the protagonist.

Trials in the past, which are alluded to in the first paragraph, remain a mystery for most of the novel. Explanations of any kind do not come until more than halfway through the text, and then in just these two instances, when the protagonist assesses her present relationship with one in the past: "This was so unlike the last time, the time of which I never speak" (96); "I had enjoyed the openness of consorting with an eligible man (how prehistoric that sounds!) in full view of others, after those stratagems and those returns in the early hours of the morning, weeping, my coat huddled round to conceal the clothes so hastily put on and now creased. The concealed pain, the lying morning face. I could not go through that again" (121). Frances Hinton's affair with a married man is not the subject of this novel, but it does color her view of the world and influence her actions. Thus, she is adverse to using deception, values respectability, and prefers companionship to heights of passion with a man. The significance of this past affair cannot be overstated, since it reveals this protagonist to be anything but a wholly innocent, inexperienced, and virtuous figure. A lack of frustration toward her sexless and directionless relationship with the young doctor, James Anstey, might have signified Frances's sexual and emotional immaturity or inexhaustible patience and a tendency toward self-denial were it not for this past. Instead, the inference is that after the passion, drama, and sheer logistics of having an illicit affair, her pleasure in the ease and respectability of *normal* dating is wholly understandable. Whereas in the past this protagonist had been the ultimate outsider as a mistress, never meant even to exist, her relationship with James Anstey makes her an insider. Formerly invisible, Frances Hinton desires to be noticed, a desire echoed in the novel's title and her repeated words "Look at me," would seem in this new relationship to be fulfilled.

A yearning to belong or be accepted by others is characteristic of Brookner's protagonists but is perhaps most pronounced in the portrayal of Frances Hinton in *Look at Me*. At the end of the first chapter, she says that writing is a way of "reminding people that I am here" (19). By the end of the next chapter, it would seem that her wish to be noticed is granted. However, she does not earn this recognition for her short-story writing. Typical of Brookner's protagonists, Frances Hinton values personal relationships far more than career success. She is the obvious predecessor to *Hotel du Lac*'s Edith Hope whose success as a romance novelist is neither the focus of the novel nor its protagonist's real energies. Career success comes easily to Brookner's protagonists. Fulfillment in their private lives is another matter altogether.

Brookner has been heralded as "one of the most English of writers pinpointing the reticence of lonely women."[13] Yet as is evident in *Look at Me,* her female protagonists are rarely alone for long. As in the plot of *Providence,* in *Look at Me* a female protagonist seems on the brink of attaining the happiness which she believes only another person can give her. Yet even more markedly than in *Providence,* Brookner continually points to an incompatibility between the protagonist and others that is more cultural than personal. This is found in the uncomfortable pairing of non-English and English characters as well as of Brookner's protagonists who are depicted as illegitimate children without belonging and those English characters who belong but are bastards in the less literal and more colloquial sense of the word. With such a focus, Brookner is not merely writing novels of manners, but in keeping with a growing number of ethnic British writers today, from Salman Rushdie to Kazuo Ishiguro, from Hanif Kureishi to Timothy Mo, she is treating issues of nationhood and identity.

Brookner's manner of looking at English nationhood or identity is characteristic of a new generation of British writers: *outsiders* looking *in.* Although Brookner has tried to turn attention away from the foreignness of her protagonists in relation to the Englishness of the men they are attracted to by saying, "the contrast is more between damaged people and those who are undamaged," it is hard to ignore the almost formulaic pairing of outsider, or foreign, protagonists and insider, or English, men such as we find in *Look at Me*.[14]

If *nation* is understood to mean "people so closely associated with each other by factors such as common descent, language, culture, history, and occupation of the same territory as to be identified as a distinct people," then many of Brookner's female protagonists and male interests do *not* inhabit the same nation.[15] While some critics believe that "Brookner represents the old dichotomy between male and female, with men getting the best out of life," such interpretations overlook fundamental differences separating these characters and causing conflicts between them.[16] They also disregard the fact that within the context of novels such as *Look at Me* there *is* a single nation for both men and women, women that is, unlike Brookner's typical protagonist, who fit the necessary criteria of "common descent." For example, Frances Hinton is repeatedly shown in opposition to Alix, the wife of one of the doctors. Alix is not only aligned with Nick of the "hectic charm . . . immense height . . . [and] generally golden quality," who is referred to as "our all England hero" or simply "England," she is married to him, and perfectly so (37, 11, 50). Even their names suggest their pairs or similar status. Both are one-syllable forms of longer names, both of which could be male (suggesting a diminishing of gender difference in view of other commonalities). Their names are also an allusion to the last czar and czarina of Russia, Nicholas and Alexandra, which places Nick and Alix not only distinct from, but superior to, Frances Hinton; her own description of the pair supports this view: "The first time that I saw Nick and Alix together, I felt as if I were witnessing the vindication of nineteenth-century theories of natural selection. . . . [T]he fittest had very clearly survived, leaving people like Olivia and me and

Mrs Halloran and Dr Simek and Dr Leventhal to founder in repro-
ductive obscurity" (37). Alix is a powerful presence in this novel,
not the least because it is on her whim that the protagonist is
befriended and later abandoned. She also plays a crucial part in
breaking up the relationship between Frances Hinton and James
Anstey. In light of these factors, it is difficult to claim that Brookner is
merely positing men and women in a modern sex war. The opposition
between characters found in *Look at Me,* as in much of Brookner's
writing, does, however, go beyond mere differences in personality.

With Nick and Alix as its figureheads, the library in *Look at Me*
serves as a microcosm for Britain in much the way the university
serves as a microcosm for Britain, with Maurice Bishop as the figure-
head, in Brookner's *Providence.* A second similarity to *Providence*
lies in the ill-fatedness, foreshadowed in this passage, of any endur-
ing or deep bond between such distinctly dissimilar persons as
Frances Hinton and Nick and Alix. The Darwinian parallels would
even suggest that such a bond would go against not only human
nature but nature itself. As a result, although the second chapter ends
with the protagonist's optimism—"Some friends change your life,
and although you know that they exist somewhere you do not
always meet them at the right time. But now the road ahead seemed
easier. I had been rescued from my solitude; I had been given another
chance; and I had high hopes of a future that would cancel out the
past"—the subsequent chapter points to the inequality inherent in
any such relationship, an inequality based *on* the past, or background,
that may not be so easy to "cancel out" (36).

The passage in which Frances Hinton identifies herself with
Olivia, Mrs. Halloran, Dr. Simek, and Dr. Leventhal, is significant
for another reason. For the factor common to them all is an outsider
and/or foreigner status. It is suggested that the two researchers, Mrs.

CAN'T BUY ME LOVE

Halloran and Dr. Simek, come in daily to the library principally to escape the cold outside. In addition, as her name suggests, the Irish Halloran is a foreigner in England, as is Simek, who is first described as "an extremely reticent Czech or Pole (we are not quite sure which and we do not see that it is our business to enquire)" (10). Frances Hinton's reluctance to enquire further into Simek's background may be interpreted as a sign of middle-class English politeness. It also, however, reflects certain Western prejudices, not against Poles or Czechs particularly, but Eastern Europeans generally as a form of bastardized or special-case European.

Since *Look at Me* predates the fall of the Berlin Wall, this view could be seen as Cold War based, but it does in fact have precedents in the pre-Communist era. The words used to describe Dr. Simek echo those in one of the most significant British novels to deal with the problem of creating an Anglo-Jewish identity. In George Eliot's *Daniel Deronda* (1876), Mr. Bult describes the Jewish Klesmer as "being a Pole, or a Czech, or something of that fermenting sort" (284). Inherent in both descriptions of East Europeans is a blurring of distinctions between nations, which is in marked contrast to the clearly stated Englishness of other figures.

As national distinctions are blurred in *Look at Me,* so are individual distinctions, as if all foreigners look alike. When Alix first meets Frances and Olivia she asks, "Which one are you?" to which the protagonist replies (as if she and Olivia were twins), "I'm Frances, and this is Olivia" (49). This exchange shows the extent of Frances's identification with Olivia. This is especially significant because, although Frances is associated with marginalized women (in her retired predecessor Miss Morpeth), the peripheral British (Mrs. Halloran), Eastern Europeans (Dr. Simik), and Jews (Dr. Leventhal—by inference of his name—and Olivia), it is with the Jewish Olivia that she is most closely aligned. Later, Frances's loyalty to Olivia will be read as betrayal by Nick and Alix, marking the end of their friendship with her. Although Frances's own background is never fully stated, the implication from her near twinning or sister stance to Olivia ("it has always been assumed," for example, that she would marry Olivia's doctor brother, who, like Dr. Leventhal and Dr. Simik, is called David) is that one cannot be fully accepted as English if one also continues to uphold other loyalties or identities, such as being Jewish (62–63).

When Nick and Alix appear to befriend Frances Hinton out of all the others in the library, they are effectively choosing her as the likeliest for conversion. The desire to change her is made apparent from the beginning of their friendship. "We must do something about her," Alix tells Nick (57). "But first of all we must do something about your appearance" she tells Frances (58). Although the protagonist is undisguisedly "delighted" with what she calls the start of her "new life" based on Nick's and Alix's "further education" of her, she is in fact a poor student and unconvertible by the novel's end (67). Like her friend Olivia, who is immobilized in her library chair after incurring spinal damage in a car accident, Frances Hinton is effectively unmovable. Where Alix sees this as proof that Frances is hopelessly flawed, Brookner leads us to conclude otherwise. Frances's resolve to be "quite firm on the matter" of her appearance foreshadows the depth of other convictions, such as her loyalty to Olivia, which will have irrevocable repercussions (58).

In a pivotal scene at the end of the novel, Frances Hinton's separateness from Nick and Alix and their friends is realized in her refusal to join in their ridiculing of Olivia's physical impairment and the bad manners they exhibit at a restaurant table. The setting is significant, as it highlights how habit and custom are important in designating an individual as one who either belongs or is an outsider. Frances Hinton's inability to join in the boisterous gluttony of those around her seals her outsider status. Not only can she not consume the quantities of custard that the others do, she is nauseated by the "sight of the yellow and white mass" (160). Whereas Brookner's protagonist epitomizes civilized politeness ("It was delicious but I really couldn't eat any more," she says), all around her act like animals (160). They "attacked" and "devoured" the custard, their gastronomic appetites matched only by their carnal ones, such as when a woman bends over a man's plate with the dessert saying, "More, darling. I want you to be good and strong tonight. More" (160). The fact that the man is Frances Hinton's boyfriend James Anstey and the woman is her friend only adds to the ghastliness of the situation. As E. M. Forster once said, "Food in fiction is mainly social. It draws characters together, but they seldom require it physiologically."[17] Since Brookner's protagonists are typically depicted as nearly anorexic, solitary eaters, the restaurant scene in *Look at Me* could not provide a starker contrast of two worlds and the inability of Brookner's protagonists to move from one to the other.

Hotel du Lac

"You are wrong to think that you cannot live without love, Edith."

"No, I am not wrong. . . . I mean that I cannot live *well* without it."

Hotel du Lac, 98

Since winning the Booker Prize and being made into a film for British television, *Hotel du Lac* continues to be the best known of Brookner's novels and the one most commonly associated with her work. Yet at the time it was written it marked a point of departure for Brookner. Unlike her previous three novels, which are set in England, events in *Hotel du Lac* occur almost exclusively abroad, in an off-season Swiss resort town. England appears only in the framework of brief flashbacks for its protagonist, whereas Switzerland is the setting of importance in terms of symbolism and plot.

While trips to France feature in both *The Debut* and *Providence,* these do not dominate either text. Presented more as an interlude in the lives of their protagonists, time spent in France serves most of all to highlight the situation of their lives in England. Since family constraints would seem to be the obstacle in the way of Ruth Weiss and Kitty Maule attaining happiness, going abroad should allow them a much sought-after freedom to pursue and fulfill their dreams. Yet the journeys in both novels fail to bring positive change to the lives of their protagonists. Just as Frances Hinton's brief association with a handsome couple and young doctor shows how intractable personality is, time spent in France does not diminish but shows the strength of filial duty and upbringing.

If a frequent response to Brookner's writing is that it is "depressing," her focus on the limits of individualism and free will may be the reason. Yet it would be wrong to conclude that in Brookner's view the individual does not matter. As her repeated structuring of novels around the life of a single protagonist shows, Brookner's writing illuminates the predicament of individuals who face lives they cannot change. Rather than being presented as the shortcoming of her protagonists, an inability to live precisely as one chooses is linked by Brookner to the limits of free will common to us all. Brookner conveys this theme in *Look at Me* through the affinity depicted between Frances Hinton and those who, because of physical impairment, age, or foreign birth, are relegated to lives very different from those represented by a robust, young, English couple.

Brookner continues to explore the limits of free will in *Hotel du Lac.* But the outcome is far more optimistic. A subtle shift in Brookner's writing is first indicated in the novel's Swiss setting, which signifies a move away from London and families. Even in *Look at Me,* the adult protagonist regards herself in terms of her family and is frequently referred to as an orphan by other characters. Also, she remains in her family home although she knows she is wholly out of place in an apartment complex in which all its inhabitants are twice her age. *Hotel du Lac*'s Edith Hope is shown on her own in a Swiss hotel. Her anonymity should denote personal freedom. Her single suitcase should symbolize her lack of encumbering duties and the ease with which she can move on. In these respects, *Hotel du Lac* promises a new beginning for its protagonist, a beginning which, unlike that in Brookner's first three novels, is not centered on a male figure.

The title *Hotel du Lac* differs from the pattern set by Brookner's first three novels in that it refers to a place, rather than a theme concerning its protagonist. Nonetheless, *Hotel du Lac,* as much as its predecessors, concerns a single protagonist. The setting to which the title refers in fact reflects the condition of Edith Hope's life as much as it is a place for events to happen. From the start of the novel, as the narrative progresses from descriptions of the scenery to Edith Hope's self-observations, the protagonist and her surroundings become inextricably linked. The result is the introduction of suspense, as the elusiveness of the Swiss landscape in fog prepares us for mysteries surrounding this protagonist: "From the window all that could be seen was a receding area of grey. It was to be supposed that beyond the grey garden, which seemed to sprout nothing but the stiffish leaves of some unfamiliar plant, lay the vast grey lake, spreading like an anaesthetic towards the invisible further shore, and beyond that, in imagination only, yet verified by the brochure, the peak of the Dent d'Oche, on which snow might already be slightly and silently falling" (7). The contrast between the grey dormancy of the lake and its "colour and incident" at other times will directly parallel the trouble with Edith Hope. For this protagonist, who dresses so impeccably and appears so very proper, does something so shocking that she is put on a flight to Switzerland by a friend who "was prepared to forgive her only on condition that she disappeared for a decent length of time and came back older, wiser, and properly apologetic" (8). All expectations are that Edith Hope will not only return to London chastened, but moreover her old self again before "the unfortunate lapse which had led to this brief exile" and "that apparently dreadful thing" she had done (8–9). What comes across immediately in this passage is a gulf between others' perception of the "thing" that happened and the protagonist's. Another discrepancy is introduced between others' perception of Edith Hope's *normal* character and that which she reveals on this singular occasion. Chapter 1 closes with the head of the hotel staring with equal confusion at the protagonist's name in the hotel register. His thoughts, in the form of the notebook jottings of a detective, invite even further interest in the protagonist. Here he guesses from her name that Edith Hope is not easily definable or easily placed: "One new arrival.

Hope, Edith Johanna. An unusual name for an English lady. Perhaps not entirely English. Perhaps not entirely a lady. Recommended, of course. But in this business one never knew" (23).

Hotel du Lac, like the fog-covered lake for which its hotel is named, is a novel propelled by the unveiling of mysteries. The first is, what has the protagonist done to deserve social ostracization to such an extreme? The second is, what does this say about the protagonist's character? Other mysteries relating to the backgrounds, pasts, even ages of the other single women staying at the hotel contribute to an atmosphere of expectancy and anticipation for the reader. Otherwise, remarkably little happens in this novel. Its plot moves as little as the fog. But when it does, revelations are indeed startling. Almost every observation on the part of the protagonist, a romance novelist who studies people with a writer's eye, proves false. Similarly, any view we may have that this protagonist is the inspiration for the meek heroines of her romance novels is dashed. Twice offered marriage, she twice refuses. Why? Her name, after all, may be the clue. She is not "entirely a lady," but is the mistress of a man she writes to every day while she is away, and to whom she will return in England (23). She is also "not entirely English," having been raised by a Viennese mother, aunt, and grandmother (23).

Protagonists of mixed background have featured in *The Debut* and *Providence* and will continue to figure prominently in Brookner's writing. Whether the protagonists' parentage is English and non-English and/or Christian and Jewish, feelings of being slightly out of place within one's family foreshadow these protagonists' unease in wider, adult social situations. The protagonist of *Hotel du Lac* is no exception. Although she has fame as a romance novelist and a face that people recognize from the covers of her books, she does not regard herself as a "worldly" sort of woman (22). She is a wearer of cardigans, who bears a "physical resemblance to Virginia Woolf" (8). Others just might invite her to their table in the dining room of the Hotel du Lac, but it would never occur to her to do the same. Too content to be an observer of people and too self-conscious of her lack of levity to fit in with them, Edith Hope bears many of the character traits of Brookner's previous protagonists. What makes *Hotel du Lac* stand out from its predecessors is the incorporation of so many of their features in one text.

Stylistically, *Hotel du Lac* exhibits the circular pattern that Brookner has employed in earlier novels. It begins and ends with the protagonist's writing to her married lover, David. The first is a letter in which she gives a jocular account of her friend's driving her to the airport ("Penelope drove fast and kept her eyes grimly ahead, as if escorting a prisoner from the dock to a maximum security wing"), followed by an equally colorful description of the other guests in the hotel and ending with deep-felt expressions of her love (10). The second is a telegram that first reads, "Coming home," then is changed to the single word "Returning" (184). At first glance, this circular pattern, which coincides with the protagonist's arrival in Switzerland and imminent return to England, might suggest a lack of progression or a dispiriting conclusion to the novel. But this is where *Hotel du Lac* dramatically differs from Brookner's earlier work. A closer look at the pieces of writing that frame the narrative shows marked differences that indicate a change in the protagonist's attitude and actions. The most striking difference is the change in length from many pages to a single word. The next is a difference in tone, from the letter's mask of joviality barely concealing deep sadness and anxiety to the telegram's resolute no-nonsense message. The other difference between these pieces of writing, and the most crucial, is that the telegram is actually sent, whereas the love letter never leaves Edith Hope's possession. If the letter at the start of the text shows Edith Hope to be a stoically passive person who allows herself to be put on a plane to a destiny she has not chosen and one where she spends her time silently observing the people around her, the telegram at the end of the text dispels this view altogether.

Hotel du Lac is basically about making choices. One occurs in the past, the other occurs in the present. The first is the reason for her being "exiled" to an out-of-season Swiss resort. The importance of this first choice is indicated by the many references to it that build anticipation by concealing more than they disclose. It is also shown in the devotion of an entire chapter to it. Whereas earlier there had been brief flashbacks concerning her lover, David, chapter 9 exclusively concerns the past as related by its omnipresent narrator. Beginning with the words "On the day of her wedding . . ." this chapter reveals how the protagonist decides, at the last instant, not to go through with a thoroughly respectable but passionless marriage (118). More than answering the mystery that has been steadily built around the protagonist's past, this earlier chance at marriage foreshadows a second one to come. What the reader cannot be sure of, however, is whether or not she will go through with it this time. Given events in the past, a proposal of marriage at the Hotel du Lac is given a momentousness that otherwise might not have been the case. After all, Edith Hope had been told by her married friends that "she had had her last chance" when she spurned Geoffrey (132).

One of Brookner's talents is to so subtly lure readers' interest in her protagonists through the uncovering of mysteries that the many clues she scatters throughout the narrative can oftentimes go unnoticed. In retrospect, for example, the names of characters in *Hotel du Lac* virtually predict their future, in addition to revealing their innermost character. "Edith" is a fairly old-fashioned name, more usually given to women of an earlier generation than that of the protagonist. The implication is that she is somehow out of date. Her refusal to update her romance novels, in other words to reflect the social realities of sexually liberated career women, may make her appear prudish. Yet her refusal to cater to the tastes of "those multi-orgasmic girls with the executive briefcases" is rooted in her sense of justice (28). By perpetuating the maxim that "the meek will inherit the earth" (in her books "it is the mouse-like unassuming girl who gets the hero"), she is effectively putting the world aright (28). Extracts from her letters to her married lover, which interrupt the narrative, serve most of all to remind us that this is *not* a sexually inexperienced or repressed woman. Would the latter, after canceling her wedding, have her married lover back to the house to help her finish the party champagne before making love, as Edith Hope does? It may seem old-fashioned to believe in the supremacy of romantic love over casual sex or marriages of convenience, but it increasingly makes sense coming from as unflinching a realist as this protagonist.

A quick look at the names of Edith Hope's three male love interests reveals some striking differences that help explain the choices she makes in their regard. The would-be husband whom she deserts in London is named "Geoffrey." The soft alliteration and assonance in this name should alert us to how he is flawed. "The totality of his mouse-like seemliness" strikes the protagonist when she sees him on the morning of their wedding (129). By leaving him standing on the steps of the registry office, she has spared herself (we are led to believe) seeing his "mouse-like seemliness" in bed. "Everyone [who] had said how good he had been to his mother . . . how lucky his wife would be . . . how lucky Edith was" did not suppose that this protagonist might want a husband who was at least as good a lover as he was a caregiver (119). True to her last name, "Hope," this protagonist aspires to more than that.

Edith Hope's second would-be husband is as flawed morally as the first is physically. Even Philip Neville's last name suggests there is something of the devil about him. And when he proposes to the protagonist, what comes to mind is the Faust legend. Like Mephistopheles, he comes not with a suitor's flowers, but proffering a new life. In a pragmatic tone and manner more suited to a business contract than affairs of the heart, he offers Edith Hope a marriage based on her natural virtue's being corrupted. Asked how his "doctrine of selfishness" is to be shared, he explains:

> "I am proposing a partnership of the most enlightened kind. . . . If you wish to take a lover, that is your concern, so long as you arrange it in a civilized manner."
>
> "And if you . . ."
>
> "The same applies, of course. . . . Think, Edith. Have you not, at some time in your well-behaved life, desired vindication? Are you not tired of being polite to rude people? . . ."
>
> Edith bowed her head.
>
> ". . . You will find that you can behave as badly as you like. As badly as everybody else likes, too. That is the way of the world." (166–67)

By repeatedly referring to this character as Mr. Neville, rather than just Philip, Brookner lends an air of authority to him that is confirmed seemingly by the protagonist's decision to accept his offer. Edith Hope changes her mind, however, when she finds him coming out of Jennifer Pusey's room the next morning. Mrs. Pusey's pampered life is in keeping with her kitten-like last name. The vulgar use of "pussy" to denote a woman's sex, especially in the context of "getting some" (i.e., sex), now makes the name "Pusey" appropriate for her daughter as well. In contrast to these characters' names, which have so many negative associations, the name of Edith's lover, David, has only positive ones.

Both associations with the name "Pusey" draw attention to the essential difference between these female characters and the protagonist. Whereas the former would seem to naturally draw adoration or sexual attraction, Edith Hope is the one who adores and gives herself over physically as an expression of her devotion. That David Simmonds may be unworthy occurs not only to the reader but also to her. In this, the depiction of love in *Hotel du Lac* is consistent with that in *The Debut, Providence,* and *Look at Me.* Inherent in each is the premise that love is no more rational than religious faith. Associations with the name "David" reinforce this view. In the Bible, David is the one chosen to be king. To explain this unlikely choice of a shepherd boy, we are told, "The Lord seeth not as man seeth; for man looketh on the outward appearance, but the Lord looketh on the heart."[18] Since appearances repeatedly prove to be misleading, whether it is Edith Hope who is misjudged by others or she who misreads people's ages, occupations, social status, and character, trusting one's heart might after all be more advisable. This message

CAN'T BUY ME LOVE

at the end of *Hotel du Lac* sets it apart from Brookner's previous novels about single women in love. Edith Hope may be a romantic, but in the context of this novel it is a virtue that also makes good sense.

CHAPTER THREE

What Child Is This . . .
Family and Friends, The Misalliance,
A Friend from England, and *Latecomers*

Family and Friends

The boys were to conquer, and the girls to flirt.
Family and Friends, 10

Beginning with *Family and Friends* (1985), Brookner's next four novels are about children. In the first of these, this focus is apparent from the start. The novel begins with an anonymous narrator studying an old wedding photograph. A large family group is pictured that clearly interests the narrator more than the unnamed bride and groom, who warrant the briefest of all descriptions. Referred to merely as "lifeless, figures from stock," they fail in spite of their obvious importance on this occasion to draw attention away from the rest of the wedding party, particularly four adolescent children and their mother Sofka.[1]

In the ensuing chapters, the focus never moves away from this family grouping. Instead, it moves from child to child. A pattern emerges in which each chapter is devoted to recounting the lives of Sofka's children, first as young adults, then as husbands, wives, and parents. Chapters 2 and 3 respectively concern Sofka's elder son and daughter, Frederick and Betty. Chapters 4 and 5 are about her younger son and daughter, Alfred and Mimi. Chapters 6 and 7 introduce Sofka's daughter-in-law, Evie (who marries Frederick) and son-in-law Max (who marries Betty). Chapter 8 features Sofka's unmarried children, Alfred and Mimi. Chapters 9 and 10 focus on Alfred's affair with Dolly and Mimi's marriage to Lautner. Chapters

WHAT CHILD IS THIS

11 and 12 respectively have Frederick and Mimi as their focus. Chapter 12 is about Betty and Max. Chapters 13 and 14 depict Sofka's death and her children's lives afterwards.

While this is undoubtedly a family chronicle, it is also the story of a matriarch whose dominating presence in the novel mirrors her domination of her children's lives. From the opening words of the narrative, Brookner sets a pattern in which interest in Sofka's children is precisely *because* they are her children. A contrast between Sofka's starlike quality and her children, who stand in its shadow, is evident from the way that the focus is on Sofka from the very start. "Here is Sofka" are the first words in the novel (7). What follows is a description of her dress and bodily stance, which will set her apart from her daughters. For one thing, their beauty is altogether different from hers, "curiously tubercular" in contrast to their mother's imposing and strong presence (7). For another, their positioning behind Sofka in the wedding photograph is symbolic of their inferior status to hers. The word "curiously" suggests that the daughters' tubercular appearance is physically unwarranted, the implication being that their frail looks reflect a spiritual frailty, which in fact proves to be the case. Frederick, too, is described in less than favorable terms as a "lazy conqueror" (7). Alfred, who is described as "sickly" and also "touching and doomed looking," epitomizes everything that the robust and regal Sofka is not (7). Herein lies the problem for this family. This mother is distinctly superior to her children. For the reader, at least, it will come as little surprise when her children fail to meet her expectations.

Family and Friends presents a departure from the single female protagonist novels that precede it (not until *Latecomers* [1988] would she break with this pattern again followed by *Lewis Percy* [1989],

A Private View [1994], and *Altered States* [1996]). But it also is notably Brookner's only family chronicle. Notwithstanding this, Sofka's children, Alfred and Mimi, bring those earlier protagonists to mind. Alfred bears a remarkable resemblance to the protagonists of *The Debut* and *Hotel du Lac* in that he is involved with someone who is married and as a consequence feels alone and unsettled. His lack of belonging is similarly symbolized by motifs of circular movement (frequent walks or drives in the country in search of a house to buy) and feelings of displacement even in his own home. There are also similarities to Kitty in *Providence,* for Alfred "wants to be as English as Dickens and roast beef" but turns out looking more and more like a disaffected character penned by Dostoevsky.[2] Even once he finds his country house, his Englishness is as illusory as the "imaginary dogs at his heels" when he goes for walks "aware that the inhabitants of the bungalows are watching him curiously out of their windows" (110).

Mimi, like the protagonists of *Providence* and *Look at Me,* loses the man she desires because patience, not boldness, rules her behavior. Both Alfred and Mimi show an attachment for their mother that would be wholly admirable if it were not so much an aspect of their general submissiveness. All the same, they are not portrayed as deserving their ill-fated lives. As in *The Debut* and *Providence,* Paris seems to offer opportunities and hope for the future that do not exist in England. But as Brookner has shown us before, inevitably "one's character and predisposition determine one's fate."[3]

Family and Friends is very much about the incompatibility between a mother's hopes for her children and their actual character and predisposition. This is first evident in their names. Sofka "named her sons after kings and emperors," but neither Frederick nor Alfred has any leadership qualities or ambition for greatness (10). The irony of being named after an Anglo-Saxon king is that Alfred cannot even decide on a home of his own to call his castle. In his endless search for one, he increasingly resembles the quintessential wandering Jew. Frederick's namesake is Prussian but he exhibits none of the stereotyped qualities to match. Instead of discipline, his life is one of languor in the Mediterranean sun where his wife runs a small hotel and he spends most of his time reading newspapers in a café. Having been expected "to divide the world and conquer it between them," their lives pale in comparison to Sofka's hopes (10).

Her daughters hardly fare better. Mireille and Babette (Mimi and Betty) have names out of "a musical comedy" and as such were expected "to flirt" (10). But Mimi's sobriety makes it impossible to conceive of her fulfilling any such role. In this respect, Sofka is a realist. When Mimi is asked by a much older family friend to be his wife, Sofka pushes her daughter into accepting his offer because she is under no allusions that there will be any others. Betty fares little better in marriage than Mimi. Ennui eventually pervades both women's lives, which bear so little resemblance to Sofka's hopes for them. Instead of becoming matriarchs in the image of their mother, Mimi and Betty are figures of powerlessness and sterility. Sofka's sons also do not rise to the grandeur to which she had hoped, their only ambitions being to sit quietly with a newspaper or possibly to take a Sunday drive in the country.

Second chances are rare in Brookner's novels. In *Family and Friends,* fates seem particularly to be sealed in one moment for Sofka's children. What is significant is that love plays a part in determining the lives of Sofka's sons as much as her daughters. Alfred's love for a married woman casts him on the peripheries of society, never its center. His drives in search for a house in the country symbolize his lack of a genuine sense of home. Frederick finds a home in Italy and has a wife and children. But his choice of Evie is a disappointment to Sofka, who regards the life of a hotel keeper to be beneath him. Both sons are effectively exiles because of their choices in love, one in adultery, the other in Italy.

Yet the similarities end here, because Frederick does achieve a contentment beyond the others, which is more characteristic of secondary characters than protagonists in Brookner's novels. Whereas Alfred resembles Brookner's protagonists who are involved in adulterous relationships, Frederick is more comparable to Heather in *A Friend from England* for having found happiness abroad. Betty is also comparable to those characters more often placed in direct opposition to the protagonists in Brookner's novels. For example, her boldness in running off to Paris contrasts with Mimi's acting as a messenger on her mother's behalf to get Betty to come home. Mimi's dutifulness not only marks her as unadventurous, but it also goes unrewarded when a dance instructor's son makes love to Betty and not her.

Although Sofka's sons are not placed in competition with one another, they can also be considered each other's nemesis. Cast as the "disobedient" one, Frederick, unlike Alfred, marries and literally escapes from his mother's domination. Whereas Frederick seems easily to put several hundred miles between his mother and himself, Alfred must go on "a mythic quest, as it were for the grail" before he can even move from her house (107). Alfred's driving style reveals his desperate frustration during this time. Behind the wheel of a car he is "harsh and unforgiving" (106). When he returns from seeing a property that does not satisfy him, it is "as if it were the end of the world" (107). When finally he purchases one, there is still no respite from the unhappiness that comes to be associated with displacement. Significantly, chapter 8 ends with the image of Alfred once again in motion. The question, "In what glade, in what grove, can Alfred find his peace?" aligns him more with the figure of a wandering Jew than the stereotype of a proud landowner (111). The picture Brookner draws of the neighboring children invading his garden and kitchen, and of his housekeeper's manipulation of him, give credence to Sofka's horror when she says, "It is your life" (109). Sofka's belief that Frederick deserves better than Evie and has married beneath himself is not supported, however, by any indication that he feels disappointed or by comparably negative images of his life in Italy.

Whereas Alfred and Mimi are portrayed as tragically disillusioned figures, Frederick and Betty are more typically presented as comic. Even Betty's failure to become a film star fails to evoke sympathy, for like Frederick's marriage, there is nothing to suggest it is unjust. Betty has no acting career because she has no talent. Frederick has a plain wife and an unassuming job because he has not got the ambition for anything else. The contrast to the depiction of Alfred's and Mimi's fates could not be more striking. Unrelieved by any comic touches, such as the description of Betty living in Beverly Hills, California ("One of the mean and selfish things that people do . . . is not to send her money from England"), Mimi's life is more comparable to the downward spire of her namesake in Puccini's opera *La Bohème* (156). While Mimi does not literally die at the height of her love, she does as much metaphorically when a dance instructor's son does not go to her hotel room in Paris.

If the first pages of *Family and Friends* resemble a camera pan-
ning the faces in a room, they also serve as a preview of the family
chronicle to come. Anticipation and tension are produced from the
juxtaposition of statements and questions. Typical of such a state-
ment is "Sofka is quite sincere in determining that her daughters
should be spared the humiliation of those who wait" (13). One in a
series of questions that are raised is "What happens to young
women, brought up to obedience, and bred to docility and virtue?"
(14). As each question goes unanswered, the effect is a countering
of Sofka's certainty with uncertainty. Brookner is expert in baiting
her readers from the very start of her novels, but never before or
since has she raised interest in so many characters so swiftly. As if
in reply to each question, and to show the limits of a parent's ability
to protect a child forever, each of the chapters that follows depicts a
crucial moment on the way to this knowledge.

In chapter 5, for example, Mimi is seen suffering the humiliation that Sofka most wanted to spare her daughters. Sent with Alfred
to Paris to persuade Betty to return to London, Mimi finds that she
herself wants "to defect" (69). This choice of words is significant,
suggesting desertion or, in language evoking the Cold War, escape
from a totalitarian state. The inference is that living with Sofka is
equivalent to the latter. Another meaning for the word "defect" is a
condition of imperfection or incompleteness. This fits Mimi's perception of herself as a single woman. Her realization of this comes
to the fore in Paris, where her previously unconscious "questing . . .
for that man, that alien, that stranger, that appointed one, who will
deliver her, the sleepwalker, from her sleep" becomes a conscious
endeavor (69).

WHAT CHILD IS THIS

Parallels between Mimi and Sleeping Beauty are made through-out chapter 5, which begins with her wakening "after a profound sleep" (59). She is alone, however, with no prince in sight, just as she will be when the chapter ends. The difference is that the twenty-four hour period covered in this chapter begins with Mimi "devoid of fear" and finishes with her having "intimations of the most absolute horror" (59, 71). What Mimi experiences in the hours in between is a loss that marks a passage from childhood innocence to maturity.

Physical violation, whether the loss of virginity or rape, is out-side the sphere of Brookner's writing. What is found instead is the internalized life, that which is frequently without witnesses. Mimi's loss is wholly intangible but no less real as a result. After telling Frank Cariani the name of her hotel and that she would be there all night, she waits for him to go there and make love to her. By morn-ing, she is still waiting and assumes that he has gone to her sister's hotel instead. The fairytale fails to end as it should, in spite of her purity and patience. In fact, these are just the reasons why it does not.

The meek shall *not* inherit the earth is the message of Brookner's novels. In *Family and Friends* this takes the particular form of the phenomenon that the good child is not always happiest. Alfred is miserable having to spend his birthday acting as a messenger for his mother. Mimi is devastated by the cruel parody of sexual awaken-ing that is her sleepless night waiting for Frank Cariani. The inno-cence and youth of these characters coupled with the fact that they are in Paris strictly on Sofka's orders contributes to an image of them as children. The fact that by sending them on this errand Sofka inflicts pain on them shows the inability of a parent to always protect a child from harm.

Reinforcing this message are the instances in the text in which parents are at least partially successful at saving their children from harm. Betty's future husband, Max Markus, is an example of a "child" who owes his very life to parent figures. In this respect, he is given more depth than his flippant manner might suggest when viewed through the eyes of his uncle. Here, in just a few sentences, Brookner conveys the extent to which even a surrogate parent can take on the role of protector and how that too can be both burdensome and impossible to fulfill completely: "This troublesome nephew, whom he dislikes but who is the son of his beloved sister, has been wished on him, there is panic in Europe, a fact of which Betty is unaware, and a general desire to reach America. 'Take him,' Margit had pleaded. 'Take him with you.' And he had taken him. But the boy is insolent, quick-witted and hysterical, perhaps already unhinged by the separation from his home" (91). Supporting this point, the next chapter begins with Sofka's answering her door to find Irma Beck, an old friend, reduced to selling lacework after fleeing what by every inference is unmistakably Hitler's Final Solution. Told that they agree not to speak of the past, it is evoked nonetheless by references to something "too dangerous, too painful," with the propensity for causing "collapses" (99). Yet the woman is released from her tragic stance when she can say about her children, "Safe. . . . Here" (99).

Although Brookner's novels frequently depict inverted parent/child relationships in which protagonists care for parents and go uncared for themselves, this is not the case in *Family and Friends*. Even the stories of secondary characters such as Max Markus and Irma Beck contribute to a vision of a world order that may be reeling from the upheavals of war but stays firmly in place at home.

Although claustrophobic at times, Sofka's home in Bryanston Square represents a reprieve. Even the limits to which Sofka can protect her children do not detract from the example she sets in trying to do so. This goes beyond her actual children to the extended family that comes to include Irma Beck and two orphaned refugee girls, Lili and Ursie.

When Sofka dies, these girls are described as crying "out of control . . . all night" as "broken, [they] relive their history, their earlier losses" (177). The image of them greeting "their banished ghosts" with their cries further evokes the Holocaust (177). This has the effect of placing Sofka in a context beyond merely the negative stereotype of a Jewish mother. There is no denying that her particular desire to keep Alfred at her side fits the picture of a smothering mother. But her willingness to let go of Frederick adds another dimension entirely. The implication from the following passage, concerning her decision to agree to his marriage to Evie and move to Italy, is that she has her children's best interests at heart: "Evie's papa has warned her privately of conditions in Europe and what they mean for families such as theirs. Wars, and rumours of war. Let the children scatter, let them put down roots, let them transplant. Sofka knows that they are safe enough for the time being. But she also knows that she can never go home again" (82). With returning to Germany out of the question and life in England uncertain, "marrying out" both figuratively and literally offers a prospect of survival.

In the absence of any god, a Darwinian view of the world pervades Brookner's novels. This is what directs Sofka's actions. Predisposed from childhood to independence, Frederick and Betty are the obvious choices to go off on their own. Alfred and Mimi stay by their mother, as much out of devotion to her as from their inability to follow in the others' footsteps. The scene in which Mimi goes into a hairdresser's in Paris only to emerge moments later with her hair unaltered, perfectly captures the difficulties of executing even seemingly superficial transformations. In Brookner's novels, however, getting one's hair cut is always a symbolic act and one that is complexly associated with cutting one's ties to family, responsibility, and the past. Mimi can do none of these. Similarly, Alfred cannot have an affair in the same way as his brother. Asked about the possibility of altering fate, Brookner has said that "character and predisposition" are what matter.[4] In *Family and Friends,* both are recognizable even from a photograph, even from childhood.

While Alfred and Mimi are more positively drawn than Frederick and Betty, who in later years appear incredibly child*ish* in their pleasures, especially Betty "in her childlike clothes, eating concoctions that might have been devised for a child's party," Brookner refuses to make them wholly virtuous figures any more than Sofka (184). Yet this does not contribute to a view of the world as defective so much as realistic. As a book reviewer for the *Spectator,* Brookner has equated the proportion of virtuous characters in a text with its propensity for sentimentality.[5] In this respect, no such charges can be raised with regards to *Family and Friends,* any more than to Brookner's other novels. Where Brookner has been accused of sentimentalizing families, it is not proven but linked to the "depoliticization" of women's concerns, focus on character and relationship, and protagonists' "resignation to things as they are."[6]

Scenes with the highest potential for sentimentality are noticeably unsentimental in Brookner's novels. Yet Sofka's deathbed scene with the family assembled around her is deeply moving. The focus on the rituals of mourning (the covering of mirrors, rending of clothing, etc.) turns attention away from the feelings to the responsibilities of Sofka's children and the previously undisclosed fact that this is a Jewish family. When Alfred reads from the Bible that Mimi's husband hands to him, "A virtuous woman who can find? Her price is above rubies," this contributes to a scene of ritualized mourning more than any attempt at glorifying Sofka's image.

Ending the novel with another wedding photograph as opposed to this death scene further eliminates any charges of sentimentality that could possibly arise. And here once more, there are children. One in particular, "Vicky (Victoria)," is the focus of attention because of her "imperious stare, so unlike a child, so like Sofka" (187). If this were a movie, another would follow in its path, proving once more that the child is, proverbially speaking, father of the man.

The Misalliance

> Blanche saw the child and mentally appropriated her
> before she knew her name: Elinor.
> > *The Misalliance,* 37

Children rarely stay children for very long in Brookner's novels. Either they are rushed into adulthood by the adults around them, as happens to Ruth in *The Debut,* or the depiction of childhood serves merely to foreshadow the adult lives of protagonists, as is the case in *Providence, Hotel du Lac, Family and Friends,* and other novels to follow. *The Misalliance* is an exception, for it features a child character who remains a child throughout the text. Although Elinor Beamish is not the protagonist, she is a key figure whose presence proves to be a catalyst for the protagonist's actions.

Elinor is an enigmatic character who is the focus of the protagonist's attention throughout the novel. Although she has nothing
physically wrong with her, she does not speak. In place of dialogue,
Brookner gives the protagonist's perceptions of the child, which
range from physical observations to imagining what the child thinks
and feels. Given that the first sentence of the novel is "Blanche Vernon occupied her time most usefully in keeping feelings at bay,"[7] the
protagonist's interest in the uncommunicative Elinor would seem to be
for a kindred spirit. This would particularly seem to be true because,
like Elinor, Blanche is an oddity in many people's eyes.

Bertie, Blanche's former husband, blames her "eccentricity"
for the break up of their marriage, and the word recurs repeatedly in
the narrative in relation to Blanche. Her attitude when he leaves her
for a woman twenty years his junior confirms this view to others as
well. An absence of "madness or rage" made it "difficult to sympa-
thize with her" (26). Her seeming acceptance of the situation makes
people ill at ease with her, much as Elinor's unresponsiveness does
(26). However, the narrative reveals that she is devastated by her
divorce. Left alone in late middle age, she finds that unlike a widow
she is "entitled to none of the world's consideration" (5). Feeling
that she has been unjustly treated, she wants to proclaim, "I am innocent . . . I always was" (5). In order to keep herself from doing just
that, she assembles an illusion of calm, which is symbolized by her
respectable dress being likened to a suit of armor (7). Ironically,
though, this serves only to alienate her further because, "she irritated
many people, particularly those who were anxious to pity her" (46).

What draws Blanche to Elinor is what the former believes is
their similarity to one another. She sees the child's refusal to speak
as a form of rebellion against "the world which she perceived as
abnormal, unsatisfactory, deficient" (47). Rebellion for Blanche

takes the form of not conforming to the conventional image of an abandoned woman. Instead of making scenes, she concentrates her efforts on giving an orderliness to her days to make up for the disorder in the world that her divorce epitomizes for her. In Elinor's "steadiness" Blanche believes there is "a desire for an ordered structured universe" much as she herself desires (47). Blanche's decision to live well in spite of her divorce—remembering her mother's maxim that this was the "best revenge"—is reflected in the symbolism that she attaches to how the child eats a slice of cake (46). Comparable to the image of Ruth as a child replacing a cup in its saucer in *The Debut,* the image of Elinor's "determined manoeuvres with the spoon" suggests more effort than is usual, and a significance beyond itself (48). Blanche sees this as a sign of the child's refusal to allow "the disappointments of life with so incompatible a parent to break down her dignity" (48). As Skinner points out, "Blanche's sense of identification with Elinor resonates throughout the novel."[8]

Speaking of the not altogether positive reception to *The Misalliance* in Britain, Brookner contends that the "bad reviews were partly a dislike of Blanche, and of me since I'm supposed to be all these women I create."[9] Although viewed by Bertie and others as eccentric, Blanche's penchant for talking about books that no one has read and frequent reference to pagan gods and nymphs is not considered amusing but dreary. The reason for this is because her sense of moral superiority keeps surfacing in all of her social interactions. If she is not amusing, this is because she does not intend to be. Instead, she puts people in their place, such as when she admonishes her friend Patrick for refusing to help Sally because his analyst advised against it. "I wish I could have an analyst who would stop me doing things like this," Blanche said. "Is she very expensive? She sounds as if she is worth every penny you pay her. By the way, what does Sally live on? No, don't answer that. She is like Danae with the shower of gold. Money falls from the sky" (129).

Elinor is similarly dreary, not because she fails to be amusing but because she tries to be. Like Blanche, Elinor behaves well and as a result goes unnoticed. Even the moment when Elinor finally breaks her silence occurs outside the narrative, as if to reinforce Blanche's opinion "that even that historic moment had passed without due recognition" (186). Sally's response when asked what her first words were compounds this view: "Oh, I don't know," said Sally. "Something about Grandma. Going to Grandma. Something like that. I forget" (185). Speaking or not, Elinor remains a lackluster child whose only saving grace is that her independent nature makes her no bother.

In complete contrast, there is Sally Beamish, whose last name suggests sun and warmth and whose bright flowing garments evoke images of Mediterranean brilliance as opposed to grey London skies. Blanche and Elinor are associated with dimly lit rooms, shadows, and rainwear. Elinor is first shown wearing a cheap looking raincoat, which, with her grave demeanor, makes her anything but appealing. Sally, on the other hand, is expensively and fashionably dressed in a kimono-style coat over layers of cotton through which her gold-bangled limbs are described as "swimming" (38). The child's drabness virtually serves as a backdrop to heighten Sally's splendor. Above all, their contrast to one another reminds Blanche of the difference between herself and "those nymphs who had seemed to mock her progress through the Italian Rooms of the National Gallery on long slow April afternoons" (40). Blanche's view that Sally belongs to a world beyond her own is supported by Patrick when he says, "I feel she was not made for the harsh realities, such as you and I must face" (128). But whereas Sally's talk of parties makes Patrick "wistful" for a life he can only imagine, it helps fuel Blanche's sense of moral superiority (128).

Patrick and Blanche are two of a kind—respectable, methodical, and lonely. But whereas he is attracted to Sally, Blanche regards Sally's presence as proof that the world is divided into unrespectable and respectable women, that is, between Sally and Bertie's girlfriend Mousie and Elinor and herself respectively. Comparable to Alix in *Look at Me,* Sally has an air of superiority that Blanche believes is unsubstantiated by any evidence of high moral character. In contrast, Blanche, like Elinor, is characterized by good behavior. Yet this fails to make either of them attractive or appealing figures. Even Brookner calls Blanche "a prig."[10] Similarly, Elinor's unobtrusive behavior may be less a matter of obedience than her lack of imagination or desire to act otherwise. The mundanity of her first words contributes to such a view.

Were this merely the story of a childless, recently divorced middle-aged woman's longing for a family, it would be banal given the colorlessness of Blanche and Elinor. But Sally and Elinor are immediately perceived by the protagonist as more than mere daughter and granddaughter figures. They serve as a catalyst for Blanche to reexamine her life in relation to the rest of the world. Reflection of this kind is a recurring feature in Brookner's novels. In *The Misalliance* it is arguably what saves Blanche from being too boring to care to read about. This protagonist's conclusions are too insightful to justify dismissing this novel as a study in the loneliness of dull people.

Although *The Misalliance* begins with the start of Blanche's relationship with Sally and Elinor and ends when the relationship does, Blanche's reflections go beyond merely the significance of this mother and daughter pair to her life. From this brief interlude, Blanche realizes truths about life that a lesser protagonist would not. These concern the nature of love and can be summarized as follows:

1) Loving someone does not mean that the person will love you back.
2) The child/parent bond is unlike any we elect for ourselves.
3) Love and possessiveness go together.
4) Love is not easy.

"The Misalliance" of the title, which at first appeared to refer to the pairing of the hedonistic Sally with the stoical Elinor, proves to be between Blanche and Elinor. Although Sally is not Elinor's biological mother (she died a month after Elinor's birth), she is nearer than Blanche to having a blood tie with the child. Brookner's earlier novels often present family ties as a burden, particularly for children. But in *The Misalliance,* however ill-matched Sally and Elinor might seem with the parent acting more like a child than the child, their bond is nonetheless irreversible.

Blanche's acceptance that she is once again alone would be a defeatist end of the novel if she were not shown as actively seeking a new start to her life. Reminiscent of Ruth in *The Debut,* Blanche "went into the hairdresser's and had most of her hair cut off" (186). Seeing this as a "symbolic action [that] seemed to demand others," she informs the hospital where she had volunteered and her house-keeper and former sister-in-law that she is going away (186). Knowledge and power go together, it would seem. *The Misalliance*

may not be the most colorful of Brookner's novels, but the mute
child who captivates its protagonist makes this one of her most
philosophically engaging and inspiring.

A Friend from England

Your place is here.

A Friend from England, 155

There are no children in *A Friend from England,* not even one as
seemingly wise beyond her years as Elinor from *The Misalliance.*
Yet Brookner's seventh novel is very much about children, specifically daughters, and filial duty. The moral territory is reminiscent of
The Debut and, to a lesser extent, *Providence,* but it would be mistaken to suppose that Brookner is merely reworking the themes of
these novels. Here the focus is on the relationship between daughters and parents as opposed to women and men. Love is seen in
terms of devotion, not romance, the fulfillment of responsibilities,
not desires, sacrifice, not gain. This set of perspectives reflects the
protagonist's view of the world that permeates this first-person narrative.

Rachel Kennedy is thirty-two years old and single. She also
likes it that way. Before the novel's publication, Brookner described
its protagonist as "an extremely emancipated young woman" whom
the critics "will *not* be able to think is me!"[11] However, it is difficult
to ignore the similarities to previous protagonists who have been so
identified with their author. Once again we see a comfortably well-
off, middle-class Londoner whose careful dress, speech, and habits
suggest a methodical rather than impulsive nature. Never found in a

pub, let alone clambering home after a few too many, Rachel epitomizes "good" behavior. Yet, comparable to Ruth in *The Debut* and
Edith in *Hotel du Lac,* she is not above falling in love with a married man. The seeming incongruity of this transgression with her
otherwise moral behavior is smoothed over by an outward demeanor
of perfect respectability. What Rachel learned from this experience
that comes to color the rest of her life is, according to her, "to see to
it that I was the one in control."[12]

Similar to Blanche in *The Misalliance,* Rachel envisages "control" less in terms of determining the direction of her life than in
determining how she is to react to its consequences. In words that
could almost have come from Blanche in *The Misalliance,* Rachel
explains her life thus: "Yes, I am brave. I've learned to be. I've
learned a lot of lessons. . . . I've learned to keep my life to myself,
not to belabour others with it. I've learned not to back myself against
the world, because I know the world will win. Always. I've learned
caution, politeness, what you call deceit, but what I call good manners. I've learned how to be alone and to put a good face on it"
(199). In keeping with all of Brookner's novels, self-revelations of
this kind are found in the final pages of the text, occurring only after
a relationship comes to an end. In *A Friend from England,* the protagonist's "goodness" is shown to be a mere facade after she fails to
convert a somewhat younger woman to her form of filial duty. In a
confrontation with Heather (nowhere the vivacious figure that Sally
is in *The Misalliance,* but similarly placed in opposition to the protagonist), Rachel realizes how misguided her attempts have been to
change someone to fit her own ideals. Yet unlike Blanche in *The
Misalliance* who, as she herself recognizes, "had made no difference"
to Sally and Elinor, Rachel does make a difference in Heather's life

WHAT CHILD IS THIS

(185). However, it is not the one that she intended. Telling Rachel that she has not failed but in fact "succeeded beyond all expectations," Heather explains that this encounter and one several months before had supported her conviction to live her life as she pleased (198). Seeing Rachel as epitomizing life at its most loathsome and cynical, Heather leaves London more certain than ever of the rightfulness of going to Venice to live with her Italian lover.

In a departure from the pattern set in Brookner's other novels, the ultimate moment of self-realization for the protagonist of *A Friend from England* is verbal, not visual. Whereas in *Hotel du Lac,* for example, the sight of Philip Neville emerging from Jennifer Pusey's bedroom convinces Edith how wrong she would be to marry him, Heather's words forever alter Rachel's view of the world. As Brookner's protagonists go, Rachel is also one of the most verbal. Her shock is thus less internalized than would be the case for other protagonists. For anyone even faintly frustrated with these protagonists' forbearance towards seemingly less worthy characters, Rachel's first confrontation with Heather is a welcome respite. Realizing that Heather has no intention of remaining in England to care for her mother following her hospitalization, Rachel tries without success to change her mind.

On hearing of Dorrie's plans to undergo what is supposed to be "a small cosmetic operation," Rachel immediately thinks the worst (130). In contrast to Heather, who shows as much gravity during hospital visiting hours as she might at a child's tea party, Rachel's sobriety suggests that she is the more concerned of the two. Indeed, Rachel can appear to be acting more like a daughter than is Heather. But a closer look at what prompts such a fierce reaction tells us more about Rachel's past than her affection for Dorrie. The evening after

Dorrie's visit, Rachel spends alone in her small apartment above her bookstore. Unable to eat, she sits as if immobilized by the "shadow of illness," which she says "darkened" her room (131). The memory of her parents' illnesses virtually becomes a ghostlike presence that made her "start up in horror," she says (131). The exact nature of her parents' illnesses is never disclosed. But the extent to which Rachel remembers it as *her* ordeal as much as theirs is obvious from the start. With the words "I rehearsed it all," the focus is on the part she sees herself as having to play in Dorrie's illness. Medical procedures or the actual effect of illness on the body are not the horror she recalls, but those rituals that precede them such as packing "presumptuous nightgowns into the suitcase, as if those fine materials might remain unsullied by the blood and waste that would certainly issue" and making "the final appointment with the hairdresser" (130). Illness is also regarded in terms of those who will remain at home and eat alone between hospital visits when "enormous courage [was] needed to make all those obligatory jokes" (130). Courage is seen in loved ones as much as in the ill themselves putting "a good face on things" (130). As a result, illness is shown not merely to have consequences for those who are ill but also for anyone who is close to them. In the case of ill parents, children would thus bear the greatest burden of anyone.

Throughout the novel, Rachel speaks of herself in terms of her relation to her actual parents, or to Oscar and Dorrie. Her sense of being adopted by the latter in order to provide a "suitable companion" for Heather aligns her again with daughters (15). Having no other image of herself than as a daughter, Rachel anticipates her role as one in Dorrie's ordeal. But when she is kept from Dorrie's bedside by the hospital staff *and* kept in the dark concerning the seriousness of Dorrie's condition, Rachel's lack of real belonging is made apparent to her. No amount of good "daughterly" behavior can make Rachel any more than a family friend. Similarly, no lack of filial devotion can alter the Livingstones' view that Heather is "a good girl" any more than it can alter the fact that she *is* their daughter (183).

In line with all of Brookner's novels, *A Friend from England* ends with the end of a relationship. Here it is between Rachel and the Livingstones as opposed to one with a lover, among a group of friends, or between a young mother and her child. Yet, as in previous novels, this relationship is revealed to have had considerably more significance for the protagonist than these others. This much is clear from each protagonist's reflections once the relationship comes to an end. What Rachel finally realizes is reminiscent of what strikes Blanche at the end of *The Misalliance:* "She had made no difference to them" (185). Yet these relationships do make a great difference to the lives of Brookner's protagonists.

The greatest irony of all in *A Friend from England* is that Rachel, who was meant to act as an older sister or mentor, actually learns about life from Heather. Comparable to the end of *The Misalliance* in which Blanche finds the "wisdom of Elinor's instincts amazed her into an admiration," *A Friend from England* shows Rachel admiring Heather's instincts for survival (185). Having learned that Heather is resolute in her plans to remain in Italy and will not return to care for her aging parents, Rachel reflects in spite of her dislike of Heather that to "strike out and claim one's own life, to impose it on others, even to embrace a caprice, was, though monstrous, sometimes admirable" (200). Moreover, Heather's selfishness would make her "acceptable" in ways that Rachel's compromises and sacrifices would not. Whereas Heather would be admired, Rachel would be pitied, as she is by Heather in this final scene.

The protagonist of *A Friend from England,* unlike those of *The Debut, Providence,* and *Look at Me,* appears perfectly content with her single status. The absence of any romantic interest in the narrative adds to this impression, as does her advice to Heather to forget about marriage altogether after her first one fails. By the novel's end, however, Rachel regards her life in strictly negative terms. Having no partner, she sees the future as "empty" and "silent" (204). She sees herself as "endangered," much like a species headed for extinction (202). Comparable to how, in *Look at Me,* Nick and Alix strike Frances as vindicating "nineteenth-century theories of natural selection," Rachel finally regards Heather as fitter for life than herself (37).

While Rachel is shocked by her conclusions, readers may be less so. From the start of the novel that introduces an orphaned protagonist and the adored only child Heather, Brookner presents these two female figures as polarized. Yet while Rachel is presented as being superior to Heather in terms of maturity, morality, and intelligence, she is also said to be frail and fearful. Rachel's aquaphobia remains a seemingly incidental detail until the end of the novel, when it comes to epitomize her general fear of making a life for herself. In her second and last confrontation with Heather in which Rachel again espouses filial duty over individual desires, the protagonist is faced not only with an uncomfortable social situation but her worst nightmare. Heather has chosen to live in Venice, a city built on water. Any strength in Rachel's arguments is thus undermined by her fearfulness in surroundings, which Heather perceives as both beautiful and liberating.

Thus water becomes equated with Heather, as do those things it symbolizes: life, mobility, even joy (as in the Biblical "my cup runneth over"). It is particularly significant that Rachel's last image of Heather is of her walking down the "Calle de la Vida," or Street of Life. In contrast to Heather, who fits in so well that she seems regularly to disappear into her surroundings in her flowing black clothes and gold jewelry, Rachel literally collides with the rubbish on the streets in her panic to keep back from the water. Rachel's dream of drowning further symbolizes the contrast between her capacity for independence and Heather's. As Brookner's "emancipated" protagonist realizes, she was in fact "dependent on the lives of others" because she lacked the necessary qualities to "invent a life" for herself.[13]

Not since *Hotel du Lac* has Brookner employed a setting to such symbolic effect as here. Few cities are also as intertextually packed as this one. With allusions to works ranging from Henry James's *The Aspern Papers* (1888) and Thomas Mann's *Der Tod in Venedig* (*Death in Venice,* 1912) to Ian McEwan's *The Comfort of Strangers* (1981), *A Friend from England,* which begins in "humdrum circumstances," is thus transformed by its Venetian setting into something altogether more dramatic and complex than would at first appear to be the case (9).

The first intimation of foreboding arises from the image of Heather, ordinarily an extremely cautious driver, nearly running over a child in the street while talking about her fiancé. When Rachel meets Michael, something about him immediately strikes her as odd, particularly in terms of his ostentatious shows of affection to his father but absence of any toward his future wife. Rachel's suspicions, however vague, of a fraud being perpetrated are confirmed when she sees Michael with a party of men at a bar where Robin, her gay coworker, asks to meet her. Michael is wearing women's makeup. In common with Thomas Mann's and McEwan's "Venice texts," death and homoerotic elements combine to build dramatic tension in *A Friend from England.*

When a death of the spirit, as opposed to an actual death, occurs at the end of *A Friend from England,* Rachel's fear of a future alone suddenly takes over other fears. "Without a face opposite mine the world was empty; without another voice it was silent," she concludes (204). Expressed in terms of the absence of someone to witness or mirror her life, this choice of words is significant because water has just this reflective property. Venice is thus equated by Rachel with that which is both feared and desired, coming face to face with herself and having another face opposite her own. Heather represents both in Venice, but in their most negative aspect. Significantly, it is after waking from a dream of drowning that Rachel realized Heather's "look was one of pity" (204). This sentiment has less to do with Rachel's single state than her philosophy of life that has made it so. It is summed up in the sentence, "I long ago decided to live my life on the surface, avoiding entanglements, confrontations, situations that cannot quickly be resolved, friendships that lead to passion" (62).

Introspections of this kind do not occur with great frequency in this narrative. When they do, however, water is nearby. After giving in to pressure from Robin to confront her phobia by going swimming with him, Rachel's thoughts similarly turn inward. Her reasons for avoiding introspection significantly enough evoke images of water. Thinking is equated with "sinking deeper" and "a wave of sadness" (62). Conversely, living on the surface level of life provides safety. Given this context, Rachel's preference for having casual affairs instead of marrying epitomizes her fear of emotional intimacy. Although in a time of AIDS more risk is usually associated with multiple partners than monogamy, in common with all of Brookner's protagonists Rachel's concerns are not physical any more than they are material.

Although she is cast very much as an observer throughout most of the text, the move to a Venetian setting marks the point at which Rachel becomes the focus over the Livingstones. After Heather disappears down the Calle de la Vida, Dorrie dies, and Oscar declares he is going to live abroad, it comes as little surprise then that the novel ends. With the Livingstones gone, life itself, as their name suggests, is effectively over for this protagonist.

As the confrontations with her nemesis Heather reveal, Rachel is no more a model of positive individuality than of freedom and maturity. From staying single and having affairs, to her attraction for the Livingstones, fear more than conviction appears to motivate her. Fear of loss makes her avoid commitment. Fear of being on her own makes her seek out surrogate parents. The "shock of truth" that strikes Rachel in Venice is that, lacking Heather's abandon, she "would always be dependent on the lives of others" (203–4). While the Livingstones had always struck this protagonist as childlike, it is in fact Rachel who is the eternal child. Too lacking in independence to make her place, the best she can do is to act according to her place in other people's lives.

Latecomers

On the train we saw a children's transport, a compartment full of small children with cardboard labels

round their necks. Their names and the names and
addresses of their recipients were clearly written on
them. It was a heart-rending sight. The children,
reduced to human parcels, already looked like
orphans.

Desider Furst, *Home Is Somewhere Else*

Rule one: never speak German.

Eva Figes, *Little Eden: A Child at War*

The transport of children from the Continent to Britain in the 1930s
and 1940s is, like the evacuation of children from London to the
countryside, a well-documented fact. What Brookner succeeds in
doing in *Latecomers* is to give the figures a human face. She does so
without historicizing or dramatizing her subject. Instead, the trauma
of these events is conveyed through what one of the protagonists of
Latecomers calls those battles "fought in the mind."[14] Brookner's
eighth novel is undoubtedly one of her most psychological. It is also
the most obviously Jewish in its concerns.

A Jewish past, or more precisely the self-censoring of a Jewish
past, is the basis for Brookner's seemingly least typical novel, in
which not one but two protagonists are male. *Latecomers* is about
two Englishmen, both called Thomas, who share a Jewish background, child refugee beginnings in London, secret use of a forbidden language (German), tortured boarding-school days, orphaning,
a successful business partnership, and an intimate lifelong friendship. Yet for all that their lives do run a parallel course, their atti-
tudes toward their lives differ just as the terms "survivor" and
"latecomer" that they would apply to themselves differ.

WHAT CHILD IS THIS

Where Thomas Fibich is preoccupied with a past he cannot remember, Thomas Hartmann is dismissive of looking back. Moreover, the *way* these characters speak reveals differences in the way each perceives life. Fibich speaks with "difficulty," just as he lives his life with difficulty. Hartmann speaks with ease and matter-of-factness, much as he would appear to live his life. Had Fibich "sighed," given his introspectiveness and sense of loss, one would read sadness. Hartmann's sighs, as they precede his advice to look forward not back, advice he has given Fibich repeatedly throughout the years, are more an expression of weariness with Fibich's preoccupations. *Latecomers* could be reduced to a comic study of two personalities, were it not for the events leading up to their going to Britain. Instead, *Latecomers* is an extremely somber Holocaust piece chronicling the lives of two Jews living in contemporary Britain.

Nonetheless, any description of Hartmann or Fibich cannot help looking like nothing but gain compared with the tremendous losses generally associated with Holocaust survivors. Each is happily married and has a child. Neither has any financial worries but can look forward to retiring well and with the satisfaction of having been a highly successful business entrepreneur. Nonetheless, Fibich in particular is a heartrending figure whose ostensibly good life is an emotional void until he can come to terms with his past. Although he is spared the fate of his parents in the Holocaust, he is not spared its legacies.

Chief among these is guilt. Recounting the moment when his parents sent him on a train to England and safety, Fibich says fifty years later, "I should have gone back. . . . I should not have left. I should have got off the train" (223). Yet Fibich's declaration of guilt comes late in life when the age of those parents could feasibly make them his children and their child his grandchild now. The simplicity of his words in these three short statements might resemble a school primer, but their message is distinctly that of an adult, not a child, speaking. The effect of each sentence beginning with "I" in conjunction with the active verbs is not only to convey the speaker's resolute feelings, but also to imply that it was the speaker's responsibility to have acted. This, of course, is a distortion of the actual situation, in which the child (Fibich) would traditionally be perceived as subordinate to and dependent on his parents. Coming at the end of the text as it does, this admission signals a departure for Fibich from the child to the adult, one that makes his words, not the event itself, climactic, which was disclosed in more vivid detail earlier in the narrative.

By regaining the past, even through memory, it is both saved *and* the loss is confirmed. Henceforth, a person can be free to look to the future. Fibich travels to Berlin with just this goal in mind. For until Fibich regains any memory of his childhood prior to being sent to Britain, he is effectively unable to proceed from that childhood to maturity. Friendship with Hartmann, though ostensibly one between equals, frequently casts Hartmann as the dominant figure. For example, Hartmann tells Fibich to put the past behind him, advises him about marriage, and leads him quickly out of the restaurant where he starts to break down. As he admonishes, advises, and tries to protect Fibich, Hartmann is repeatedly depicted as a parent figure.

Proof that Fibich has acquired a new maturity as a result of regaining some memory of his past is that the roles that he and Hartmann had had appear reversed afterwards. Not only does Hartmann start to think about the past until Fibich scolds and, in so, doing rescues him,

WHAT CHILD IS THIS

Hartmann also submits to Fibich in the manner in which Fibich had always previously submitted to Hartmann. It is also revealing for the way in which Fibich seems to have finally learned the lesson that Hartmann had for so long tried to teach him, and the one Hartmann conversely seems to have forgotten. It is as if Fibich's newfound maturity has freed Hartmann not only of his pseudo-parent role, but also of being ever briefly the child again. Significantly, Hartmann's memory is set in the home and features two domestic, even maternal, figures, his housekeeper and nurse.

Given that both Fibich and Hartmann left Germany as young boys, it might be expected that their memories would feature parents or parent-type figures. Given that both men were orphaned, it might also be expected that such memories would be painful to recollect, reminding them of what was lost. It comes as no surprise then that Fibich's memory of the very moment when he was separated from his parents is traumatic to recall. It is the dramatic point of departure (literally and figuratively) from one world to another, from danger to safety, and in all likelihood from death to life. Indeed, death is foreshadowed in the image of his mother fainting when she says goodbye.

What Hartmann remembers is mundane by comparison. There is no action, no conflict, no scene. He merely remembers the names of his housekeeper and nurse. One might ask why Brookner sets up this contrast in recollections. Is its purpose to show that Hartmann is himself mundane and that Fibich is superior in some way to him? As a result, is Hartmann's loss meant to be read as less than Fibich's? The meagerness of his memory, heightened by the short, simple sentences in which he conveys it, is in direct contrast to the image of "Hartmann, a voluptuary," introduced in the first words of the novel.

Hartmann's recollection signals a departure for him in several regards. It is the only time that he confesses to thinking without censorship about the past or uses the words "remembered." Modified by the words "I have just," Hartmann's recollection is comparable to Fibich's in that it is found suddenly, without effort, after many years.

In both cases, these memories tell us more about the men than the women who are remembered, because the women's role is foremost a symbolic one that is in keeping with common notions of national identity and gender and epitomized by the vocabulary of nationalism (motherland or home). The significance of these women-centered memories for Fibich and Hartman is not to fill out a picture of the past, but to provide from the past an indisputable sense of belonging that can carry over into the present and change them for the better.

For Fibich, change is depicted particularly as a release from fear. When he says, "I should have gone back. . . . I should not have left. I should have got off the train," the boldness of these statements, although only whispered, is unprecedented (223). Previously Fibich was a figure characterized by fear, as suggested by the frequency with which forms of the word were attributed to him. A "frightened modesty" and "fearful toothaches" epitomize his childhood (9). Groundless worries about having enough to eat and other less definable fears pervade his life, something which Brookner conveys with an uncommon use of repetition ("He feared the future. For as long as he could remember he had feared the future") (32).

Hartmann, whose adopted sense of English self-control and discipline makes him seem more preoccupied with avoiding public embarrassment than showing concern for a friend, appears altered after he recalls the names of his nurse and housekeeper. Vulnerable to a lapse of nostalgia, Hartmann suddenly appears less in control and more human, which is in direct contrast to his earlier manner, which is distinctly one of control and seeming lack of human compassion. Is his fear of social embarrassment for Fibich or himself? The indefinite pronoun "he" in the sentence "A collapse here, in Durrant's Hotel, where he lunched every day?" is distinctly ambiguous (224). When the tears continue to fall down Fibich's face, we would seem to be left in little doubt. "On my account," he says. "We have to go" (224). Hartmann's composure, coupled with the anger that we are told he feels, suggests that his concern is predominantly for himself.

Beyond what their responses to the past reveal about Fibich and Hartmann, however, Brookner's juxtaposition of such seemingly opposite memories serves one purpose above all. Whether what is remembered is extraordinary or ordinary, horrific in nature or more like trivia, it is precious for ever having been remembered at all because it gives a sense of identity and belonging to the bearer. The juxtaposition of the drama of Fibich's recollection with the mundanity of Hartmann's indicates as much. Without the latter, the predominate theme of *Latecomers* would be survivor guilt above and beyond the complexities of having combined British and Jewish identities. With the inclusion of Hartmann's memory of his housekeeper's and nurse's names, *Latecomers* becomes a story of exile according to the Hebrew meaning of *Galut*, "which denotes a tragic sense of displacement (where the migrant is essentially the passive object of an impersonal history)," as opposed to *Golah*, which "implies residence in a foreign country (where the migrant is in charge of his or her own destiny)."[15] What both memories essentially bring to their bearers is a momentary sense of control over the past and sense of home and belonging that are lacking in their lives in Britain. Prior to remembering their boyhoods in Germany, even the luxury of homesickness is denied them.

While it can be argued that *home* "can only have meaning once one experiences a level of displacement from it," without memory even this benefit is lost as the absence of any concept of home in the lives of Fibich and Hartmann illustrates.[16] Although both men marry and have children (Hartmann even has grandchildren), they seem surprisingly displaced in what one would regard as their homes. And rather than affirming their identities as husbands and fathers, the children who come displace them even further by their difference from them. "It would have seemed, to a stranger coming into the room for the first time, as if Marianne, the docile, the silent, were Christine's child and Toto Yvette's (68)." As a result, the presence of Toto serves to unsettle Fibich by making his own home feel foreign to him. Brookner refers to this son's arrival as an unbargained-for "disruption" and "alienation" in Fibich's mind that surpasses that which might traditionally be perceived by a first-time father (70). This son, whose "very being was foreign to him," makes Fibich's home an unsettling place, almost as alienating as Toto's presence is to him.

In Brookner's novels where the protagonist is a single female, the longing for romance as a respite from loneliness has been, perhaps justly, used by critics as proof of the protagonist's passivity. In *Latecomers,* where the protagonists are both married and male, such claims would seem out of place. Yet there are similarities in that Fibich, especially, lacks a firm sense of belonging. To Fibich, what "in his view, incapacitated both Christine and himself and constituted their inalienable but unwelcome bond, was that they had been deprived of their childhood through the involuntary absence of adults, that his own parents and Christine's mother had vanished without a trace, spirited away by a turn of events that wholly excluded their offspring, without being known, and that they had left been left in the charge of strangers who, though tolerably well disposed, were uninvolved, uninterested" (129). Whether it is an abandoning lover or parent, or both as it happens in *Providence,* the effect is the same on Brookner's female and male protagonists. Like Fibich, they are emotionally "incapacitated." Consequently, anything that can be construed as rejection by the protagonist has considerable impact. Thus the foreignness and inaccessibility of Toto brings to Fibich's mind other rejections, intended or otherwise, such as his parents' abandonment of him. The injury also mirrors realities of Fibich's life in Britain, in which, of course, the foreigner is not Toto, but Fibich. Problems of "understanding" bring to mind the language difficulties that Fibich first faced, in addition to a difference in temperament that set Fibich apart from his British counterparts. Regarded by Fibich as "a foundling" in their midst, Toto mirrors Fibich's own foundling status upon arrival in Britain (73). Yet Toto is not the outsider that Fibich was, not merely because he is described as a "facsimile Englishman," but because he undermines the sense of belonging of those around him as Fibich did not (81). Finally, Toto's lack of resemblance to either his mother or father raises the questions, "Whose child is this?" and "Who are we?"— questions that might not be so disturbing if Fibich's own sense of identity were not already an issue. However, identity is an issue *because* it is in crisis.[17]

The particular disharmony between parents and child is between the seemingly weak Fibiches and strong Toto, or "infant Hercules," who is given to days of "superhuman activity" (67, 74). This parallels the stereotyped differences separating Jews and Gentiles, or what, according to Nazi ideology, are "two demiurgic figures. The Aryan, who achieves his finest embodiment in the German race, represents beauty, creativity, and above all strength [and] the Semite [who] is incapable of creation or even conservation."[18]

Toto is not only repeatedly associated with having strength (seemingly beyond that of his parents), but also a "gift of beauty" that made him "so astonishingly handsome that his parents often wished for a more ordinary-looking son," for he "looked extremely English, but it was the kind of Englishness that has something legendary about it, that cannot be matched up with known prototype, which flatters fantasies with an aura of ancestral perfection . . . [which] had nothing to do with the realities of Toto's ancestry" (78, 79). He is also given to creative activities, which his early interest in Yvette's application of makeup foreshadows and which is later realized in his choice of an acting career. Fibich and Christine stand in virtual opposition to Toto. Lacking in energy, strength, beauty, or creativity, this couple, who considered themselves barren before Toto is conceived, consider "themselves to be in the wrong" once he is born (74). Feeling inferior in comparison to their son, Fibich and his wife see themselves as the source of disharmony. Thus Fibich's wish that he had gone back to his parents on the train platform sounds less selfless than self-serving. For there, where the lines of difference were drawn according to Jew and Semite, there would have been a harmony in which he at least would have no doubt where he belonged.

WHAT CHILD IS THIS

For Fibich and Hartmann, the past means childhood. Or more precisely, *childhoods*. Even without actively remembering their German childhood, it is ever present, as it intrudes on their English one. For any recollection of their English childhood is marked by their outsider status as foreign refugees. As a result, one childhood would seem to outweigh the other in significance and consequence, which larger historical events prove. Beyond anything else, Jewish parentage makes the lives of Fibich and Hartmann what they are. The importance of one's birth in determining the future is an integral feature of Holocaust literature and an underlying theme in all of Brookner's novels. As the last in a series that have children or childhood as the focus, *Latecomers* is also the most optimistic. The letter that ends the novel, a letter from Fibich to his son, is comfortable and confident in tone. No pain is attached to either the present or the past. Also for the first time, Fibich exhibits a maturity that lends special significance to the signature "Your loving father, Thomas Manfred Fibich" (248). As his middle name, which was his own father's name, suggests, Fibich has finally come of age as a man and a father. In contrast to the truths that many of Brookner's protagonists uncover, the one that Fibich leaves to his son—that some battles are "sometimes won"—is optimistic indeed.

CHAPTER FOUR

Happily Ever After?
Lewis Percy, Brief Lives, and *A Closed Eye*

Lewis Percy

> One trails all sorts of things around with one, things that simply won't be got rid of.
>
> *Lewis Percy,* 213

Although marriages feature in all of Brookner's novels, with *Lewis Percy* (1989) they become the focus. Brookner's ninth novel is about a failed marriage, how it begins and how it ends. In between, there is a brief and emotionally consuming, though physically unconsummated, affair. But even before then, it would seem that happiness does not come easily or in great abundance to the husband in this tale. In this regard, the protagonist of *Lewis Percy* bears a striking resemblance to the single female protagonists of Brookner's earlier novels. Although this is the first of Brookner's novels to feature a single male protagonist before *A Private View* in 1994 and *Altered States* two years after, there is more that is familiar than unfamiliar in *Lewis Percy*.

To begin with, Lewis is an only child soon to be orphaned when his fragile mother suddenly succumbs to an unspecified illness, which makes her waste away before his eyes. Even before this, however, the absence of a father and painful recessiveness of his mother make Lewis an "emotional" and "intellectual" orphan.[1] His love for her is matched only by his sense of duty to look after her, sentiments that he later transfers to his wife. The problem is that they are reversed where Tissy is concerned. His feeling of responsibility outweighs any other emotions. While this may sound like a prescription for marital disaster, Lewis sees things differently. Effectively converting his grief for his mother into an interest in the childlike librarian to whom he returns his mother's books, he envisages in Tissy "a way of life that would be appropriate without imprisoning him in false expectations."[2] Marrying her would also be in keeping with Lewis's view of the world. This is reflected in his studies. Before meeting his future wife, he is finishing a thesis on "the concept of heroism in the nineteenth-century novel" (3). While studying in Paris, the attraction he has for the hypochrondriac and lackluster Cynthia shows also that he is drawn to women with "invalid sex-appeal" (7). The connection, however tenuous, between Tissy and his mother increases his estimation that he is doing the right thing. If anything, Tissy should be the perfect match for Lewis.

The only child of a widow, Tissy, like Lewis, works in a library and is quiet inside and out of it. The soft consonants of her name, like Lewis's, suggest more similarities than differences between them. Suffering from agoraphobia, she is ushered like a virtual invalid to and from the library by her mother. That is, until Lewis starts to walk with her. The practical problem for any would-be hero is to find someone in need of rescuing. To this end, at least, Tissy is the perfect object of desire. The overbearingness of her mother and a shady doctor companion (Dr. Jago, as in *Iago,* Othello's lying friend?) even suggest that her condition is being worsened, if not altogether invented, by those around her. Lewis quickly concludes that the less Tissy is with them—and more with him—the greater her chances are of leading a normal life.

Whether or not her health is as delicate as her mother and doctor claim is just one mystery that surrounds Tissy Harper. She speaks little. Her eyes, which "were basically without expression," give nothing away (94). Lewis is curious about her "inner thoughts and reflections" but, having no idea "how to gain access" to them, accepts her as an enigma even after they are married (95). But her impenetrability thrills Lewis for only so long, before it starts to become oppressive and makes him look forward to leaving the house to go to work.

Lewis is among many of Brookner's protagonists who find comfort in books and a virtual refuge from life in libraries. There, where "the rules were so clear, so reassuring, and so manifestly without guile," he can momentarily escape the uncertainties he feels at home (98). Given Lewis's love of order, something that is evidenced by his patience with the job of updating the index card catalogs, Tissy should be the perfect partner. As Lewis himself admits, Tissy is an exemplary wife in terms of her housekeeping. Likened to an archeologist at an ancient tomb, Tissy treats their home, which had been his mother's, as a depository of objects to be recovered, polished, and displayed. Daily "excavations" result in their home becoming "a small marital museum, virtuous with household tasks, punctiliously performed" (93–94). But orderliness is not Lewis's only passion, and herein lies the major source of conflict in this marriage.

Sexually speaking, this is a marriage of opposites. Throughout chapter 7, Lewis is described being willing to wait for Tissy "to come to life" (98). But certainly she has already done so almost overnight in terms of taking control of the house and gaining an air of self assurance and maturity that she had never had before. Yet the transformation that Lewis longs for is of a more intimate nature. What he is waiting for is the flowering of this childlike wife into a full-fledged woman in bed. While his "embraces were permitted and even indulged," Tissy's lack of responsiveness strikes at Lewis's masculinity (96).

Although there are no scenes with Lewis and Tissy actually in bed, so many allusions and references are made to Lewis's disappointment in this regard that a picture can easily be drawn. Tissy's unresponsiveness and passivity come across in Lewis's unsatisfied yearning for any sign of passion or initiative from her. "He longed," Brookner writes, "for her to overwhelm him, to seduce him, or even just to surprise him. But nothing came, and he was too puzzled ever to allude to this disappointment and too good-natured ever to complain about it" (96).

The staidness and respectability of this marriage are in stark contrast to the youthfulness of this couple and the fact that the "swinging sixties" have long since hit Britain. When, for example, Lewis goes into the library his boss greets him with the word "peace," to which he replies "Good morning" (124). There is even an encounter between Lewis and a pot-smoking student. When Lewis throws him out of the library, it is to exclamations of "Jesus, man, this is 1970" (125). If Lewis is cast as an establishment figure in such encounters, this is not to say that he is wholly out of step with the spirit of the times. He simply lives according to rules and order. When it is morning you say "good morning." When you are in a library you do not smoke. Thus, when he buys Tissy miniskirts, it is because "fashion now dictated that the wide-skirted dresses should be put away" (97).

The effect on Tissy is nothing short of dramatic. With Lewis's prompting, Tissy is transformed from a matronly librarian to a Twiggy look-alike with her "thin legs," "knock kneed stance," short blond hair, and big eyes (97). As people start to notice her attractiveness, Lewis at least has this satisfaction. Out walking with her, he feels proud, "and told himself that he was now in truth a married man" (97). The choice of "married" instead of "lucky" is significant, suggesting that this marriage needs validation not that it is good, but that it exists at all. The line of thought that follows further suggests that physical intimacy may hardly even exist between these two: "His reward would come later, when his wife was confident enough to shed her wifeliness. At the same time he warned himself not to frighten her with his ardour. He had waited so long that he could wait a little longer before coming into his own" (97). Once again the implication is that Tissy, who should confirm manhood, is denying Lewis his. At one point, Lewis even imagines that her fastidiousness is a form of teasing seduction, "a brilliant form of delay" until she grants him gratification (98).

Brookner frequently discloses her characters' sexual appetites through their gastronomic ones. The final restaurant scene in *Look at Me* is perhaps the best example of this. Frances's inability to eat with the same abandon as Alix and Maria convinces them that she is unlike them and undeserving of James's attention. Similarly, Tissy's sparrow-like appetite comes to reflect her difference from Lewis in more ways than one. The dishes that she serves are characterized by a lack of excitement and sauces that are "always a little too thin" (105). The parallels to Lewis's depiction of Tissy in bed are almost too obvious to mention. She is also unexciting and perhaps too thin. Lewis's conclusion that he "had more feeling for food than she did" foreshadows the ultimate revelation to come that he had more feeling *for her* than she did for him.

When Lewis's friend Pen and his sister Emmy come to dinner, the correlation between an appetite for food and for life in general becomes most apparent. Not only does Emmy eat "enthusiastically," but her exclamations over the meal reveal that this is not a woman who does things halfway (121, 122). When one of her earrings falls onto her plate, she removes them both with such panache that even Lewis cannot conceal his delight. When Tissy misses Emmy's plate and drops a roast poussin onto the tablecloth, Emmy takes over the serving at once, then declares, "Nothing is better than food. . . . Not even sex. Well, not all the time" (122). The greatness of Emmy's appetite is matched by the extravagance of her dress, the masses of jewelry, and voluminous Mexican robes. Yet, unlike Sally Beamish in *The Misalliance,* Emmy has a heart to match her grand presence. The first indication of this is her attempts to make Tissy feel at ease. There is even something innately motherly in the way she hugs Tissy and wipes away her tears when there are spills. Above all, Emmy's most striking feature is her seemingly infectious exuberance and sense of delight. She makes Lewis grin whereas Tissy prompts Lewis to take her hand as if "willing her to enjoy herself" (120).

When Lewis next sees Emmy, food is again a center of attention reflecting their similar temperaments. Filling in for Pen, who had promised to take Emmy to lunch, Lewis finds himself whisked off to an impromptu picnic. Once more, Emmy appears superior to Tissy purely because of her propensity for spontaneity. Watching her shop for their picnic, Lewis is again struck by how much she is unlike his wife. "Her attitude to food seemed to be temporary, festive, far removed from the rendering of raw materials that engaged so much of Tissy's time," Lewis reflects. "This lunch was more in the nature of a children's party" (133). Whereas this image from childhood is a positive one, those that Tissy inspires are more ambiguous. By the end of their marriage Lewis realizes that Tissy is not childlike but childish. When he concludes that she "had never grown up" he means this in the very most negative sense (240).

Lewis's attraction for Emmy proves to be a catalyst for change both in Tissy and their marriage. Although Lewis never actually goes to bed with Emmy, his desire for her is too obvious for him to deny to either Tissy or Emmy. With his wife, more goes unsaid than said. Lengthy passages of unspoken thoughts are followed by the single word or two that Lewis does dare to utter. Very often it is no more than an incomplete utterance that goes unanswered or the calling of Tissy's name. With Emmy, however, Lewis has no chance for deliberation before he speaks. Her spontaneity, which he had previously found so attractive, leaves him "unprepared" (153). Yet at the same time, his refusal to go to bed with her catches her unawares. The result is some of the lengthiest dialogues in all of Brookner's novels. Hard hitting and fast paced, they are in marked contrast to those between Lewis and his wife. Whereas with Tissy silence is matched by a physical stillness, with Emmy there is always some movement, such as her repeatedly walking away and Lewis's walking, then running after her. There is even an element of movement in the seeming reversal of stereotypical male and female roles when Emmy leaves Lewis as if *he* were Scarlett O'Hara and she were Rhett Butler in the Hollywood film of *Gone with the Wind*. Two years after his refusal to sleep with Emmy, Lewis professes his love for her but still shows no more willingness to act on his feelings than before. Telling him once more to "grow up," Emmy leaves him with Rhett's final words to Scarlett, "frankly, my dear, I don't give a damn" (204). Not only is her resolve conveyed by these words, they also serve to remind us that she is by profession an actress. Earlier, when she tells him that he "probably read too much," this reference to his profession as a librarian draws attention again to their differing views of the world and backgrounds (203).

The attraction of opposites is a frequent feature in Brookner's novels. Whether what is most pronounced is a difference in age (Ruth and Duplessis, who is old enough to be her father, in *The Debut*), background (Kitty's ethnic mix and Maurice's Englishness in *Providence*), or social standing (Frances and the upperclass Alix and Nick in *Look at Me*), what is common to them all is a difference in morality. Only in *Hotel du Lac* is the issue of morality nearly so pronounced as it is here.

As in the exchanges between Edith and Neville, Lewis and Emmy cannot speak of each other personally without also expressing their general views on responsibility, right and wrong. Yet whereas Neville comes across as a wholly negative figure on this account, Emmy is far more sympathetic. This is because we are shown (as Lewis is) Emmy's private as well as public face. The contrast between the flamboyantly carefree dinner guest when she is first shown and the young woman crying "tears of frustration, like a child" afterwards in Lewis's arms makes her a far more complex and humane character than she might have been otherwise (136). It also makes her a more sympathetic one than Tissy.

Emmy's speech about lovers, whom she has had since she was sixteen, strips affairs of any glamor and reveals her to be a woman with intelligence and wit in spite of her disappointments in love. In this respect, she and Lewis share a secret. They give every appearance of being happy in their personal lives, yet are painfully dissatisfied without knowing how to change anything. Moreover, both blame destiny. Here is Emmy telling Lewis what it is like to be a mistress: "I wanted to be married, like you. I wanted children, roses round the door, the whole thing. The trouble is, I don't look the part, so I never got the offers. And now I'm typecast, I suppose" (136). Just as Emmy sees herself as locked in the role of mistress, never a wife, Lewis wishes he could play the part of the hero. Regarding Tissy as his "quest," Lewis prepares "to lose all" if there are gains as well (56). But as Emmy could have told him from her own experience, gains are not guaranteed. What precisely Lewis expects from marrying Tissy has less to do with any particular vision of the future with her than with his own vague notion of becoming a hero as a result. The absence of any such transformation is the source of his discontent. Once married, he finds that he not only was "not a hero, never less," but that he was "just a man" (104). To make matters worse, he finds marriage is no escape from feelings of loneliness and unease.

Lewis's long walks, like those of so many of Brookner's protagonists, are symbolic of his desire for escape and reflect a marginality even at home. The latter is especially made apparent when he first walks home from work and finds Tissy's mother and doctor there, full of reproaches for his unexplained lateness. When Dr. Jago strokes Tissy's hair and cheek, Lewis is shocked by the intimacy of the gesture, as if this too usurps his position at home. Unable to remove the image from his mind, Lewis lets Tissy go to bed ahead of him as if conceding that any real intimacy with her is beyond his reach.

What immediately follows in the opening words of chapter 8 further suggests that this is true. Letting her hair grow out, Tissy "reverted to her original appearance": "virginal gentility" (108). Her emotional and physical remoteness is conveyed with her likeness now to "a ghost" (108). Mirroring their estrangement is how they eat

at separate times in separate rooms, Lewis from "a plate in the oven,
like a message in a tomb" (110). Although Lewis still holds onto the
hope of teaching Tissy "to be happy," by the end of chapter 8 any
chance of this seems gone (111).

It is in keeping with Lewis's contemplative nature that his
"adultery" with Emmy should be more a matter of desire than
action. Nonetheless, its ramifications are just as great. Losing his
wife and the child that they eventually have, this protagonist does
seem to pay most dearly and disproportionately for what is a transgression merely of the mind. Other Brookner protagonists who com-
mit adultery (and there are many) get off much easier. But the end
of *Lewis Percy,* however ambiguous, allows some room for a happy
ending. The final image of Emmy running onto Lewis's plane
moments before he is about to set off for a new life in America can
be read as the perfect reunion scene. Now free of Tissy, Emmy
could be his. Another reading, however, that Lewis's hopes for a
new start in America may be thwarted by Emmy, is based on the
scene's similarity to the end of *The Misalliance.* The sudden arrival
of Blanche's ex-husband on the eve of her going to Paris might foretell a new start for them together or a return to the mistakes of the
past. Similarly, the arrival of Emmy could signal "a new destructive
cycle" for Lewis.[3]

In either case, happiness is envisaged abroad, not in England.
This is a recurring feature of Brookner's novels, one that indicates
the existence of social concerns beyond the strictly personal dramas
of protagonists. When, for example, Lewis returns from his studies,
London strikes him as incredibly dark compared to Paris. The
"poor" light is more than climatic, but symptomatic of the difference
in temperament between the two nations (15). Deciding that "the war

cast a longer shadow" in England than on the Continent, Lewis perceives the reluctance to complain as a form of patriotism (15). It also
fits the stereotype of the English as having a stiff upper lip. In this
regard, Lewis responds to his nation like an outsider, taking literally
the casual expressions "Mustn't grumble. Can't complain" (17). It
also reflects his view that in fact there is something to complain
about, the modesty of life. Later, when his marriage turns out to be
as modest and lacking in excitement, he reverts to type. He is "too
good-natured ever to complain about it" (96). Herein lies Lewis's
problem. Part of him feels at home in the atmosphere of a French
salon and between the pages of romantic novels. The other part, "the
peaceable part, the part that had always been attuned to his mother's
widowhood, and her fidelity, and her undemanding nature—perhaps
in particular the latter—led him to accept the idea of life that was not
all excitement and gusto, but rather give over to what was expected
of him, to meditation, and to repose" (16). Balancing these two
strains in his personality is as difficult as Kitty's attempts to balance
two separate lives, one English and one French, in *Providence*.
Where Tissy's modesty makes Lewis long for passion, Emmy's
immodesty makes Lewis act like a prig. The contrast between the
two women in his life mirrors the incompatibility of the two strains
in his character. Like "things that simply won't be got rid of," Lewis
trails around with him an attraction both for disorder and order as
represented by Emmy and Tissy respectively (16). Given the failure
of his marriage to Tissy, the prospect of a relationship with Emmy
faring any better is very much open to question, thereby making the
ending an ambiguous one. Comparable to other protagonists bur-
dened by aging parents and unfashionable backgrounds, Lewis is

bound both by his mother's modest upbringing and the romantic visions of the world he reads about in books.

Brief Lives

> All one needed was a pair of dancing feet, a pretty
> face, or a singing voice which would captivate the
> man of one's dreams and secure one's heart's desire.
> *Brief Lives*, 15

In the second of Brookner's novels about marriage, literature at last has a reprieve. In *Brief Lives* (1990), Hollywood is to blame for its protagonist's misfortune. As the daughter of a cinema manager, Fay Dodworth finds her life "shaped" both physically and morally by movies.[4] The ones that make a particular impression on her are the romantic comedies of the late thirties and early forties. In fact, no other reality seems to exist for this protagonist. Rarely has a childhood and young adulthood been as idyllically depicted as this one. The now elderly Fay's nostalgic tone of reminiscence in this first-person narrative contributes to a view that the "the naive 1940s to the wised-up present day" were a "fall from grace."[5]

The Great Depression and Second World War certainly never seem to intrude. Only one reference is made, and obliquely, to "sights which should never be seen by anyone, man or woman" (16). Given that movie going is virtually the only context of experience, "sights" might refer to newsreel images rather than those directly experienced by the protagonist. Yet even if we are to understand this to mean the horrors of the concentration camps that were captured on film after the war, the protagonist contends that it did not "entirely shatter" the "innocence" of her generation (16).

While Brookner is typically more concerned with the interior rather than exterior lives of her protagonists, the exclusion of historical and political events from this narrative contributes to the impression that Fay is an innocent throughout much of her life. Since the world for Fay hardly extended beyond the elderberry tree at the bottom of her garden or the latest movie at her father's cinema, nothing leads us to expect that she should be any wiser or more worldly than she turns out to be. If this protagonist is to be faulted for her trust in romantic ideals, then "a generation or two of young men and women" should also be (16). The unexceptionality of Fay is something that is conveyed very strongly in the opening two chapters. The impact of the movies is presented as a phenomenon that Fay shared with anyone her age. In this respect, the protagonist of *Brief Lives* seems far more ordinary and mainstream than other Brookner protagonists. Nothing in the narrative builds a picture of a figure whose outlook or behavior sets her apart from others or makes her lack belonging. On the contrary, Fay is no different from most anyone her age growing up in Britain during the thirties and forties. Thus the story that unfolds is elevated from a singular experience to one that might be representative of a generation. Events are more comprehensible and valuable as a result.

If nothing, not even the Second World War, could "entirely shatter" this protagonist's state of innocence, then what could? The third chapter begins with a flashback to Fay's first meeting with her future mother-in-law and the beginning of her loss of innocence. To Fay, Lavinia Langdon is incomprehensibly cynical. Just as Fay is too naive to see "the makings of a rather brutal success" in her future husband, she is too inexperienced to understand how anyone could be a cynic—even a mother-in-law who "came from a family of runaway husbands: her own father defaulted, before her husband" (26). What is foreshadowed in this first scene between Fay and "Vinnie," as her mother-in-law prefers to be called, is the shattering of Fay's own innocence at the hands of a man. Where Henry Langdon ran off to Spain with his mistress, Owen will desert Fay in other ways.

Brief Lives differs from *The Misalliance* and others because the significance of events is conveyed not only in the final pages, but from the start of the text. Nonetheless, understanding comes to the protagonist only after a relationship has ended. In this case, the death of a friend makes the protagonist think back over the past. From the opening words of the novel, "Julia died," the first focus is Fay's friendship with Julia. The first chapter is devoted to Julia, with paragraphs beginning either with the name "Julia" or simply "She." From the start, the fact that Fay and Julia were friends at all is presented as a paradox. The fourth sentence in the text reads: "I never liked her, nor did she like me; strange, then, how we managed to keep up a sort of friendship for so long" (3). An element of mystery, of something not easily explicable, is conveyed with the word "strange." Moreover, the inference is that it is a mystery to Fay as well. Thus the opening words of the narrative set the tone of the chapters to come. Events are not depicted as being dramatic in themselves. Instead, the drama is in the conclusions that Fay draws from them once she starts looking back.

The opening paragraph is typical of many that follow. The tone is one of detached calm, which appears compatible with a subject of such seemingly little consequence as a casual friendship. But with the second chapter the focus turns to Fay, her childhood and the

ideals she carries over into adulthood. Chapter 3 continues chrono-
logically from there to the day of Fay's wedding to Owen. Julia is
not mentioned again until the end of chapter 4. The effect of
recounting Fay's first meeting with Julia four chapters into the text
rather than at the start lends interest to an otherwise ordinary social
encounter. Yet dinner parties, even just for two, are never without
significance in Brookner's novels. Sitting at a table with others features regularly in scenes of acceptance and rejection.

Cooking disasters often go hand in hand with disastrous relationships, such as the burnt offerings that Ruth in *The Debut* gives
to a young man before she meets Duplessis. But as David Galef points
out in the essay, "You Aren't What You Eat: Anita Brookner's
Dilemma," this dinner's failure is not from her "lack of culinary
skill; rather because she fails to take into account the careless, post-
prandial arrival of the egotistic male" and "confused his acceptance
of food with an offer of love."[6] In *Providence,* Kitty similarly con-
fuses Maurice's enthusiasm for a meal with an enthusiasm for her.
As for Edith's cholesterol-laden fry-ups that David so adores in
Hotel du Lac, surely his remarks that he never gets to eat like that at
home point to one of the attractions of this affair. Thus, even the best
of meals is no indication of the quality of the relationship. The food
is plentiful in the penultimate scene of rejection in *Look at Me,*
whereas the meagerness of the snacks at Madame Doche's are more
than compensated for by the sense of belonging that Lewis Percy
feels with his concierge in Paris. If there is one constant in the many
food-related scenes in Brookner's novels, it is that meals frequently
signal the onset or collapse of a relationship.

In *Brief Lives,* Fay's friendship with Julia begins as inauspi-
ciously as the dinner that she prepares through a haze of headache and

nausea. It finishes with praises for Fay from Owen and from Julia and her husband, Charlie. Yet apart from a brief mention that roast veal and coffee were served, no mention is made of the food itself. This is unlike Brookner, who can be bothered to describe the "melting base of pear and crushed walnut" at the bottom of a slice of ginger cake in *Lewis Percy* (63). If not the meal itself, what then made the evening such a success? Fay and Charlie appear not to speak at all, the only exchange recounted being between Julia and Owen.

Julia arrives at the dinner decidedly overdressed in black silk and flourishing a black chiffon scarf. She then proceeds to parody the middle-class housewife as a symbol of British postwar egalitarianism saying, "I want you to treat me as yourselves. Forget about Julia. Julia is no more. Let people have what they want. If they want ruffians there are plenty to go round. My day is done" (46). When Charlie takes the scarf she nonetheless continues, "What's the matter? . . . Isn't that the sort of thing middle-class housewives wear? For I suppose we are all middle-class now" (46–47). In contrast to Charlie, who out of embarrassment tries to subdue Julia, Owen openly delights in her audacity and joins in her repartee, laughing, "What about the ruffians?" (47). Julia's response, both bodily and verbally, is blatantly flirtatious. "Slowly and suggestively" she lifts her eyelids then answers, "I dare say they are available if one knows where to look for them" (47). Just as Fay and Charlie are not a part of this exchange, they virtually do not exist for the rest of the evening as far as Julia and Owen seem concerned. Although Fay is too unwell to eat, Julia receives Owen's attention and together they "ate heartily, and in Julia's case with enormous pantomimes of appreciation" (47). Julia's husband alone shows any concern for Fay, asking her if she is all right when he helps her to get the coffee (47).

The significance of this dinner scene goes well beyond being the beginning, as we are told, of the friendship between Fay and Julia. For one thing, it shows the marked opposition between the two female characters. Brookner frequently places her female protagonists in social situations with someone directly opposite in character and looks. In keeping with Brookner's other novels, the protagonist's good behavior goes unnoticed, whereas her counterpart's bad behavior wins her favor. The degree of good and bad behavior makes no difference. The result will be the same in every encounter between these two characters.

A natural compatibility between Julia and Owen, as well as between Fay and Charlie, also emerges. Whereas the latter are cast as observers, Julia and Owen are presented as the focus of attention. There is also an impression of the latter looking "up" as well as at their partners, not in admiration of any of their qualities so much as a reflection of their superior social status.

Although Fay first describes Julia as being "in the same line of work" as herself, class distinctions are apparent even here. Before marrying Owen, Fay is a singer of sentimental love songs on the radio. Julia is on the stage, being herself as much as anything. Fay uses the term "disuese" to describe her, a word for entertainer that is as dated as the form of entertainment that Julia provides (4). The speech about "ruffians" fits in with the comic monologues that made her name, but go out of style during the war when "her manner was found to be too snobbish for popular taste" (4). Whereas people had once been "amused that so obvious an aristocrat should condescend to entertain the public in this manner," the women in factories think differently and foretell a change in Britain (4). Yet Julia never changes. Instead she finds a new audience in Fay and Owen once her days of appearing in *Vogue* magazine and turning heads and stopping conversation in restaurants are done. Since from the start of the text we are told that Julia "had had a number of lovers, some of them prestigious, others quite shady," her flirting with Owen and his attentiveness afterwards suggest the beginning of more than merely Julia's friendship with Fay, but also perhaps an affair with Fay's husband (4).

Owen's own moral fiber is suspect. Fay remembers her wedding day in terms of the colors she and her mother and best friend Millie wore. The blue, grey, and pink that each respectively wore would seem to complement "the end of a beautiful spring, with the promise of a beautiful summer" (14). But the dislike that Mrs. Dodworth and Millie feel for Owen makes even these details prophetic. For the blue that Fay wears does not foretell clear skies or happiness, but disappointment and pain. The grey of her mother's dress suggests a shroud symbolic of her death in another spring and the subsequent end of Fay's idealism. Pink, with its associations with both femininity and passion, points to Millie's sustaining of both in a marriage altogether different from Fay's. Chapter 3 ends with Fay dressing for her wedding and watching her best friend's "troubled" face like a window on her future (34). While Fay has the makeup of the romantic comedy heroine (ordinary working girl, virtual orphan, with a modest singing voice), Owen also fits the hero type with his good looks, charm, and "elevated rank" (15). But whereas the cinema was "classless," therein lying its appeal according to Fay, Britain remains a classbased society (15). Like *The Debut*'s Ruth, who discovers that the moral lessons of literature do not match the moral order of the world, Fay follows a Hollywood formula for happiness only to find another ending in store for her.

Chapter 4 begins innocuously enough with, "Owen was away a lot on business" (35). Understatement and the supplying of seemingly inconsequential information are common features of Brookner's writing. Here as in other novels, however, the refusal to dramatize is characteristic of Brookner's protagonists' efforts at self-control, and even the most mundane details prove to have importance. Owen's absences, whether they are entirely for business or pleasure, look suspect once other factors lead Fay to guess that her husband's business dealings are "irregular," and that he may be embezzling funds (81). This coincides with her realization that he is anything but the perfect husband. When Owen leaves her mother's funeral early, "furious at being exposed" to Fay's "humble origins," even the facade of a happy marriage is destroyed (81).

Because *Brief Lives* is in the form of a first-person narrative, Fay is a more complex character than would otherwise be the case. There are effectively two Fays. One is young and envisages the future solely in terms of domestic happiness; the other has the wisdom of experience to know that the dreams of her youth, and a whole generation, were faulty. This is not to say that the narrator bears any resemblance to Julia. An acceptance of fate is very different from cynicism.

Julia is the latter, and frequently described as "fearless" as well. But in spite of Fay's being frightened much of the time, she acts bravely and repeatedly puts consideration for others before herself. In contrast, Julia is "dedicated principally to herself" (48). Although Julia is said to have the "fearlessness of the true aristocrat," her ridiculing of the middle classes shows her resentment of their new prominence and loss of her own (52). Linking their rise to her own fall, she exclaims, "This hatred of the upper classes! Well, I'll never be anything else. I'm out of touch. I'm finished. My day is done" (108). A bully, Julia preys on those who seem weak: her former dresser, Pearl Chesney; personal maid, Maureen; husband, Charlie; and sole friend, Fay. In actuality, they are resilient survivors. Pearl Chesney is reunited with the illegitimate son whom she could not raise. Maureen marries and moves on. And Charlie and Fay satisfy their loneliness by having an affair with one another.

Closer in temperament to one another than to their own partners, Charlie and Fay become lovers at no cost to anyone else. They are careful where Julia and Owen are characteristically not. For Fay, this is in keeping with her background, which would seem to demand better behavior than from the upper classes, represented by Julia. This divide is comparable to the one between the correctness of "a foreigner" such as *Providence*'s Kitty and the "natives, [who] after all, don't need to bother" (155).

The absence of any scenes of torrid lovemaking or impassioned proclamations suggests that the affair is based less on sex or love than the alleviation of loneliness. The china cup that Charlie gives Fay and becomes his may be interpreted as a womb symbol, indicative of the domestic comforts that are associated with Fay not Julia. The irony is that the better wife is not the better loved of the two. Of her marriage to Owen, she concludes that her "excess of feeling had amused him, for he had none of his own" (88). Coming to the same conclusion with Charlie, Fay decides to end the affair because as she puts it, "He would never leave her. He had never left her. I was marginal" (144).

The friendship between Fay and Julia is wholly uneventful. Yet interest is raised in the opening words of the narrative. Inherent in asking "how" they stayed friends is "why." The same questions could be asked concerning the two marriages that feature here. To varying degrees, duty would seem to be the one constant in all of these relationships. However, the first-person narration limits us to Fay's perspective, which is speculative at best about others' motivations. At best, Fay's part in these relationships is explained in the philosophical fashion that so frequently features toward the end of Brookner's novels. The paradox of how Fay "had always wanted to be good, yet had turned out flawed" leads her to question the extent to which "worthy actions compensated for a lack of true virtue" (167). Like Blanche who in *The Misalliance* discovers that loving cannot make someone love you, Fay realizes that good acts cannot undo wrong ones. The adultery takes her virtue just as her marriage takes her innocence. The fact that she survives both without becoming a cynic is what makes her one of Brookner's most sympathetic as well as knowing protagonists. The lengthy passages on marriage and adultery offer a perspective on the subject that, though presented as specific to women and a particular generation in Britain, is also universal in many respects. The romantic ideal of marriage, the thrill of taking risks, the problem of guilt, coping with loneliness and disappointment, the need for something to look forward to even at an advanced age, these are just some of the issues covered in *Brief Lives*.

The title may at first appear to be a misnomer. The characters in this novel all live well into middle age and beyond. Fay and Julia live on to old age, outliving their husbands, as do Fay's mother and mother-in-law and Julia's mother. The brevity to which the title refers would seem to have more to do with the periods of happiness these characters enjoy. For Fay's mother, there is effectively no life to live after her husband dies. The same is true for Fay's mother-in-law, who never recovers from the death of her son who cares for her better than her husband ever did.

Julia also is never the same after her husband's death. Refusing to go out and hardly leaving her bed at all, Julia's widowhood more closely resembles a state of invalidism. Fay also retreats indoors and hardly ever goes out. But her reasons are different from those of these other widows. As Charlie's mistress, her role is to wait for him, being never quite certain when he will call or come by. The deceit also breeds a wariness of people, so that even the most casual social contact has her fraught with with worries should anyone learn of her transgression. Most obviously this gives tension to even the most mundane exchanges with Julia, thereby lending an excitement to wholly inconsequential and everyday scenes. The impact of the affair on Fay's life outweighs its brevity, much as their marriages do for all of the female characters in the novel. In spite of its flaws, the ideal of married love permeates all of these lives, unifying all women, even as unlikely a pair as Fay and Julia. Hollywood plays its part in perpetuating some myths, but in the end Fay gives it credit for being more realistic than she had at first recognized. Rather than blame the movies, Fay faults the innocence of youth. Hope made her myopic. She could not see beyond the romantic comedies in which "when the heroine married the hero that was the end of the story, and life was justified and fulfilled" (143). Later in life, she remembers the movies differently for "when they both survive the ending the story changes. And when one of them survives or outlives the other the story changes again and not for the better" (143). These words

as perfectly sum up the story of Fay's own life and the parallel stories of loss of the other "brief lives" that touch her.

A Closed Eye

> A woman of Harriet's age should not be spending
> time with her husband and her elderly parents when
> she could be in bed with a lover.
>
> *A Closed Eye,* 201

Marriage, adultery, friendship—the subjects are familiar enough,
but the opening of *A Closed Eye* is unusual. The first chapter is in its
entirety a letter. The first words of the text are an address in the
upper right hand corner as is the format for a letter, "Residence
Cecil, Rue du Chateau, La Tour de Peilz (Vaud), Suisse."⁷ Attention
is drawn back to this address from the start of the letter, when its
author writes: "No doubt you will be surprised to hear from me after
all this time, and from such a strange place. Not that it is so very
strange: indeed, it is extremely civilized, but you probably think of
us still, if you think of us at all, in that house in Wellington Square
which you once knew so well, though not perhaps in the happiest of
circumstances" (3). The "surprise" that the letter writer anticipates
her "dear Lizzie" will feel suggests that a surprise is in store as well
for the reader of *A Closed Eye*. Repetition of the word "strange" also
helps build anticipation for the unveiling of mysteries. Among these
are, Who is Lizzie? Who is the letter writer? Why has there not been
contact in so long? Why is there any now? How long is "all this
time"? What was the house in Wellington Square? What were the

circumstances that were not the happiest? All of these questions will be answered in the course of the third-person omniscient narrative.

The benefit of introducing the narrative with this letter is the sudden intimacy with its author that it thrusts upon the reader. Because the novel begins as a letter, it places the reader in two positions—as a novel reader and letter reader, as a detached observer and the letter's recipient, as an outsider and an insider. Some letters in literary texts present a voyeuristic opportunity for the reader to become privy to more than perhaps might be in the narrative. Here, however, more is revealed by one narrational intrusion than all of its words. After Harriet Lytton recounts how her husband's poor health first took them to a clinic in Switzerland and that she has remained there and is "not at all lonely," the following words cast doubt on all that she has said: "Such lies, she thought" (4). Set apart as a separate paragraph and in parentheses, these words have a powerful effect of making the novel reader knowledgeable of more than the letter's recipient might well be. This writer is not beyond falsifying the truth.

One other set of words placed in parentheses also is significant. After the opening "My dear Lizzie," there are the words "she wrote" (3). By breaking with the letter format, Brookner makes us read the letter not as Lizzie might but from the standpoint of the omniscient narrator watching Harriet. The focus is thus placed already on Harriet, who will turn out to be the novel's protagonist. This parenthetical inclusion also serves to remind us of the physical distance between letter writer and recipient that foreshadows a repeated motif of emotional distance between Harriet and Lizzie, as well as other characters in the novel.

Where the words "she wrote" direct emphasis on the writer rather than the reader of the letter, they also draw attention to the act of writing rather than reading. For all of the seeming ease and friendliness of its tone, this directive is a reminder that this letter is a narrative with a not altogether trustworthy narrator. The reticence of the first paragraph suggests concealment. The reference to "such lies" implies a deception (4). The conditions for Lizzie's accepting the invitation to Switzerland ("One name must never be mentioned") hints at something vaguely conspiratorial, at the least a demand for silent complicity (5). The final words of the letter also suggest something that is not quite right. Following "With love, as always" are the words "Your old friend Harriet (Lytton)" (5). Comparable to the parenthetical insert "Such lies," this one also lays open to question the validity of the preceding words. If, in fact, Harriet is the "old friend" whom she claims to be and with such affection that she signs with love "as always," then why is it necessary to add her last name, and in such a way as to draw attention to it? Should it be taken as merely superfluous, the inclusion of "Lytton" would point to a carelessness in Harriet's writing. Yet everything preceding it would deny this. The prose is too finely written, poised, controlled, and correct. The incongruity of intimacy with formality and distance at the end of this letter points to a complexity in this relationship that foreshadows others to come.

The letter is also more than merely an invitation to a potential houseguest. Two other purposes are conveyed in it: to put right Lizzie's memory of her mother and to set Lizzie on the right path in life. The implication is that Lizzie's view of both is negative and self-destructive. Harriet writes, "don't let an impression of sadness dim our love of life, which is too precious to be wasted" (5). She goes on to say that she might be instrumental in correcting this: "I have always felt that you had it in you to be something remarkable, and I should like, if I may, to help you towards whatever you see as your goal" (5).

Generally in Brookner's novels it is her protagonists whom others want to change, not the reverse. Caroline's efforts to get Kitty to follow her fashion ideas in *Providence* and Alix's attempts to subvert Frances's morality in *Look at Me* are just two examples, one peripheral and one integral to their respective texts. It might seem that the pattern of one female figure's trying to make another in her own likeness is being repeated in *A Closed Eye*. But there are marked differences. For one, the transformation Harriet envisages is neither as superficial as Caroline intends nor as morally empty as Alix would have it. In addition, the offer of help that is introduced at the start of the novel is not developed further until the final chapter.

This circular pattern is employed frequently by Brookner, whether it is the device of looking at a wedding photograph in *Family and Friends* or the subject of Kitty's ethnic background in *Providence,* which is found at the beginning and end of the texts. In each, a sense of continuation is conveyed that is not always altogether positive. The same is true in *A Closed Eye.* As the letter to Lizzie illustrates, Harriet's invitation to go to Switzerland is also an invitation to return to the past, Harriet's youth, when Lizzie's mother and she were first friends. Harriet's mandate that a certain name is never mentioned and her offer to share "those early days" with Lizzie shows a selective memory at work (5). Remembering the past in this manner would seem to be a form of emotional survival, as suggested by the references to the "shock" that Lizzie has had and Harriet's own need for courage (4, 5). The power of the mind both as a positive and negative force is implicit in Harriet's words to Lizzie, revealing a person for whom self-control is tantamount to happiness.

Inherent in Harriet's offer of a vacation are her services as a mentor to Lizzie. A taste of the lessons to come are found in Harriet's words "don't let an impression of sadness dim your love of life, which is too precious to be wasted" (5). Given that this visit has preconditions of agreeing to self-censorship and selective memory, the optimism that Harriet is promoting appears contingent on "turning a blind eye." The title *A Closed Eye* evokes this saying, as does the novel's epigraph, a quote from Henry James's *Madame de Mauves:* "She strikes me as a person who is begging off from full knowledge,— who has struck a truce with painful truth, and is trying awhile the experiment of living with closed eyes." As opposed to looking at life through proverbial rose-colored glasses, Harriet looks away from what pains her. She has had to.

All of Brookner's protagonists bear the legacies of their birth, but none so strikingly as this one. On first sight, her mother feels "pity, almost distaste," and once home from the hospital is "glad to leave the child with her nurse" (16). When Harriet balks at an offer of marriage from a man as old as her father, and whom she does not love, her mother reminds her of the birthmark disfiguring her face. "And not everyone . . . Although it's faded a lot . . . ," she tells her, "crying in earnest now, ashamed of herself, bitter with impatience" (24). Her mother is correct. Not everyone can ignore it. Her girlfriends are few and advise her to conceal the mark with makeup. Male admirers do not exist. Her dates with Freddie will be her first and last. Like all of Brookner's protagonists, Harriet is obedient to a fault. Implored by her mother to "do the right thing," Harriet puts her parents' wishes before her own (23). True to her mother's words, her parents will "enjoy life" at the cost of her own (24).

If the turn of events seems unjust, this is not because the protagonist's parents are portrayed as undeserving. Until Harriet's marriage, in fact, Merle and Hughie are presented as figures of self-sacrifice. A fighter pilot with the RAF during the war, Harriet's father puts his life on the line for his country. Although he survives his plane's being shot down, he is severely disabled for the rest of his life. The terms "shell shock" or "posttraumatic syndrome" are never used. This is typical of Brookner's depictions of illness, which are no less vivid for going unnamed. This is because the focus is on the caregiver rather than the ill person or illness itself. The effect on those around the person who is stricken is thus made more universally recognizable than designating any particular disorder might be. Comparable to many illnesses, Hughie's has an impact on the entire household, which ranges from responsibilities of looking after him to keeping up a brave face. But the weight of both falls predominantly on the shoulders of Merle, who is effectively reduced to being a single mother of two—"bringing up a baby and supporting a husband who was an emotional invalid single handed" (26). The losses incurred as a result of his condition are also greatest for Merle because she (unlike Hughie or Harriet) remembers her husband when he was "dashing" (16). Merle is virtually a widow, yet devoid of the freedom to marry again. Ironically, it is Harriet's marriage that offers Merle a new start. Trapped in a disappointing marriage, Merle is nonetheless free to change homes once Harriet leaves. She learns "the prospect of spending money, after the years of careful parsimony, [which] cheered her considerably, and in a while she forgot about Harriet, for the furnishing of the new flat made her feel as if she were the heroine of an adventure, a fresh start, while her daughter, who looked on solemnly and without comment, seemed oddly static, as though the roles were reversed and she were now the adult" (27).

Reversal of parent/child roles is a common feature in Brookner's writing. This takes two forms, often in combination within one novel. Either the parents of protagonists do not care for them as children or the protagonists have to care for their parents although they themselves are barely more than children or both. As a consequence, Brookner's protagonists appear, in manner if not physically, aged beyond their actual years. The burden of such a predicament is both practical and psychological. Hindered from acting independently, such protagonists stop thinking of a future for themselves. Caregiver to her father, Ruth in *The Debut* considers her life to have been "ruined" by the literature that taught her the moral codes of behavior that brought her to that point.

In *A Closed Eye,* Harriet casts no such blame, but the losses she incurs because of her sense of filial duty are no less. Chapter 4 begins with the first of these, when she refers to her parents as "no longer Mother and Father, but Merle and Hughie" (25). As the change of names implies, on marrying Freddie, Harriet is effectively orphaned. In addition, the contrast between her life and that which Merle and Hughie embark on could not be more striking. Whereas Harriet is prematurely thrust into middle age because of her marriage, her parents regain the freedom of their twenties, unspoiled by wars or disfigured daughters.

Harriet's birth not only coincides with the outbreak of war, the implication is that her marked face is associated with the psychological scars that her father bears home with him after he is released from a German prisoner-of-war camp. Whereas Harriet's face is marred by what is there, her father's face is marred by an "absence in his eyes" (17). From childhood, Harriet learns to be "a stoic in her way" when the sight of herself in a mirror or the violent shaking of her father's hands becomes too much to bear (18). Books become a refuge. Like so many of Brookner's protagonists, she speaks French but remains most of her life in England. She also remains in a marriage in which telling the truth is inconceivable.

The first thing that Harriet can never confess is that she is physically revolted by her husband. We are told that though inexperienced, she knows "instinctively" that Freddie is "not an ideal lover" (29). Yet she considers him "an ideal husband" (29). To Harriet, the contrast between Freddie's manner by day and by night or his "doubleness" makes him a virtual Dr. Jekyll and Mr. Hyde. According to her, this respectable businessman is wholly incompatible with the figure in bed the night before.

Although events are presented from Harriet's perspective, with the result of building compassion for her, Freddie does not come across as wholly monstrous. One reason for this is that Harriet may be as lacking in knowledge as she is inexperienced about sexual matters. She is "too young for her age," in her mother's view (26). With her friends, she is often "puzzled" by their laughter, as if she does not fully understand their jokes any more than she realizes when Freddie is courting her (20). The fact that she is "amused" as well as shocked by his treatment of her in bed makes her sound like a child for whom a parent's sexuality seems similarly incredible (30). Such a response is compatible with her general attitude toward her husband, whom she "liked" because he "was more of a father than her father had ever been" (29).

What, according to Harriet, constitutes perfection in Freddie as a husband also reveals a great deal about this protagonist. To Harriet, it is his limitless capacity for devotion while expecting nothing in return except that she be "reasonable and decorative" (29). In this way, marriage satisfies her desire to remain the child whose parents "asked nothing of her, seemed glad of her presence, [and] did not enquire into her thoughts" (19). While her modesty and "lack of sexual awareness" may make Harriet a daughter who is no bother, these qualities do not necessarily make her a good wife (35). When Freddie says after they have made love, "You're not much good at this, are you?" it is clear that disappointment is on both sides (157). When he tells her, "Quiet" and "Keep still," it is evident that Freddie expects the same passivity from Harriet in bed as at other times (30). Although decidedly crude, if not brutal, in making sexual demands of her, the real source of difficulty is revealed in Harriet's fantasies about a lover who "knew her every mood, her every movement, [and] felt as ardently and sadly as she did herself" (31). Not enquiring into her thoughts, which Harriet initially considered one of Freddie's positive attributes, becomes his worst failing. This is because this protagonist *has* thoughts for the first time in her life.

What Harriet longs to speak of but cannot is her attraction for her best friend's husband. Unable certainly to tell Freddie any more than Tessa, she feels "a loneliness beyond measure" (157). This secret invests even the most casual encounter with either of these two, any mutual friends, not to mention Jack Peckham, with an element of danger. The resulting tension lends interest to one of Brookner's most defeated and defeatist protagonists. Since concealment is integral to the preservation of her marriage and friendship, inaction rather than action is paramount. As a result, nothing much happens in the novel. Even the deaths of Freddie, Tessa, and Harriet's daughter do not alter a pattern in which Harriet responds to events rather than initiating them. As is the case in all of Brookner's novels, the internalized life of protagonists is more significant than the life that is acted upon.

As in *Lewis Percy,* the fact that desires are not satisfied matters little. Their impact is still considerable. Although a marriage does not break apart in *A Closed Eye* as happens in *Lewis Percy,* the central problem is the same. How do we live with disappointment? Harriet's answer is to endure in silence. In this she exhibits an acceptance of fate that is common to all of Brookner's protagonists. But like these others, she is scorned rather than praised for her efforts. The most chilling condemnation, chilling for its harshness but also its insight, comes from her mother, who thinks Harriet would be better off "in bed with a lover" (201). Had Merle voiced her thoughts, one feels that Harriet's life might have turned out differently. At the very least, Harriet might have seemed more human to her mother. The cost of respectability is high indeed for Brookner's protagonists. Secrets demand reticence. And reticence does not help to make friends. Perhaps the greatest irony presented in *Lewis Percy, Brief Lives,* and *A Closed Eye* is that marriage, which is conventionally regarded as the end of being on one's own, can be an even lonelier state to endure.

CHAPTER FIVE

Starting Over

Fraud, Dolly, and *A Private View*

Fraud

She had escaped from a prison cell, and she was
determined never again to be imprisoned.

Fraud, 129

Beginning with *Fraud,* Brookner's next three novels all feature a
death that considerably alters the protagonist's life and offers an
unprecedented opportunity for starting over. In *Fraud* (1992), it is
the death of Anna Durrant's invalid mother, Amy. In *Dolly* (1993),
it is the death of Dolly's husband, Hugo. In *A Private View* (1993),
it is the death of George Bland's best friend, Michael Putnam. From
inauspicious beginnings, each of these novels ranks among Brookner's
most optimistic in viewpoint.

   The first of these has prompted comparisons of Brookner's
writing to Herman Melville's "Bartleby the Scrivener" (the protagonist of *Fraud*'s words "That is not what I'm looking for" being reminiscent of Bartleby's cryptic "I would prefer not to").[1] In contrast to
"Sherlock Holmes tales [which] exploit both the puzzle and the
adventure," Brookner's writing, like that of Henry James, proves
that "mysteries are not there to be solved."[2] Nonetheless, *Fraud*
begins in the manner of a detective story. The protagonist, Anna
Durrant, or "Miss Durrant" as she is referred to, has gone missing.
The case is under police investigation. But the protagonist who
might appear from such an opening to be the victim or even the perpetrator of a crime is neither. She is alive and well in Paris, having
decided to move there after her mother's death. On another level,

however, crimes have been committed. Anna's mother is swindled by a bigamist, George Ainsworth. Anna's best friend, Marie-France, is exploited by an opportunist with a roving eye, Philippe Dunoyer. Anna's doctor, Lawrence Halliday, is seduced into marriage by Vickie Gibson, who exudes sexuality but otherwise has no feelings for him. An acquaintance of Anna's called Philippa is caught in an affair with a married man who merely sees her as a recreation. Throughout the novel, people are duped and subjected to disappointment.

Whereas Anna is a witness to each of these "frauds," as she calls them, her own life goes largely unnoticed until her unaccountable disappearance. In fact, she makes no secret of her plans to go to Paris. What prompts an investigation is that Lawrence Halliday, with whom she had been in love, cannot conceive of her remaining away for so long. After she misses several appointments with him, he is sure something is wrong and calls the police. Ironically, she has never felt better.

During all the years that Anna looks after her mother, she is known for her unrankled good cheer. Yet this only serves to further isolate her. In the community in which she lives, the virtue of self-sacrifice seems as out of date as a spinster. This point is made repeatedly in the novel. At the end of chapter 1, for example, one of the policemen investigating Anna's disappearance says this about her: "Sounds a funny type. Old fashioned. Looking after the mother, and so on. Unmarried. Typical spinster, I suppose," to which the other responds, "Except that there aren't any spinsters any more, Barry. They're all up there at the cutting edge. I blame Joan Collins."[3]

Earlier in the same chapter, an elderly woman called Mrs. Marsh compares Anna to "a daughter in a Victorian novel. Little Dorrit" (11). The two literary references, to steamy romance novels and a work by Charles Dickens, could not be more in opposition to one another. The implication is that Anna is out of time and out of place. Other protagonists of Brookner's have been set apart because of their ethnicity, religion, or social background. Anna is singled out as different by characters ranging from a policeman in his twenties to the aged Mrs. Marsh solely because of her acts of self-sacrifice. To Anna, however, they are seen as acts of love. For this reason, her declaration of freedom upon her mother's death and her admission of feelings of entrapment for so long make her a noble rather than priggish figure. Yet the correlation that Anna makes between the death of her mother and a release from prison is never spoken to anyone. As is characteristic in Brookner's novels, revealing truths such as this are found in passages of introspection not dialogue. Thus, the reader sees a side of the protagonist that few others ever do.

Mrs. Marsh's comparison of Anna to Little Dorrit is significant in this respect. Where the protagonist in Dickens's novel is born in a debtor's prison, Brookner's protagonist is effectively incarcerated in her mother's widowhood with her. Anna's father having died when she was five, she lives half a century in the shadow of his absence, which is only exacerbated by the injury done by George to her mother. In both instances, the damage done to Amy Durrant is both emotional and physical, as symbolized by her heart condition. Similarly, Anna cares for her mother in more ways than one. When, for example, she learns that Lawrence is about to be married, she withholds this information from her mother in order not to upset her. Asking Lawrence to do the same, Anna is not alone in perpetrating this act of concealment. But in this, as in their other encounters, the intimacy between them is not an altogether comfortable one.

The tension between these two characters is perhaps best epitomized when Lawrence, in his capacity as Anna's doctor, gives her a physical examination. Continuing the motif of appearances differing from realities, the scene is anything but a simple showing of Lawrence at work or Anna receiving the notice of a doctor who suspects she suffers from anorexia. Their inability to look squarely at one another reveals their unease and suggests that more than doctor/patient roles are at play here. While Anna stares at a glass cabinet, Lawrence examines her body with the eye of someone appreciating a piece of art. Finding her body to be "beautiful, fine and gracile," Lawrence is reminded of a Degas painting (152). Later, the words "His hands pressed firmly down on her abdomen" would be perfectly in keeping with Lawrence's role as a doctor, except for the preceding nonmedical observations he makes. His wandering thoughts suggest that his eyes too are wandering, in a less than professional capacity, over Anna's body. Without these interpolations, the exchange that follows would be wholly innocuous. Lawrence asks, "Does that hurt?" Anna answers, "No. Nothing hurts," and then he says, "You can get dressed Anna" (152). In context, such words have considerable ambiguity. If these characters do not wholly fit the part of doctor and patient, then who are they? The questions concerning pain cannot help but be a reminder of the emotional pain that Anna has suffered on Lawrence's account. Because of this, her words may also be interpreted as being ironic.

By eroticizing this scene, Brookner makes clear that romantic interest has not only been on Anna's side. This is extremely important. Otherwise the protagonist would appear pitiable, as in other instances, for example when she received "pitying glances" from "mothers more battle-ready on their daughters' behalf than her own mother had ever dreamt of being" (45). As it happens, Lawrence comes across as pitiable and Anna as admirable. Whereas previously Anna's moral behavior made her the antithesis of women such as Vickie, now it is as an object of desire that she surpasses the other. The two are in fact connected. The overt sexual energy that first attracts Lawrence to Vickie turns out not to be connected with a zest for life or love of him, but is symptomatic of deep-seated neuroses within the family. Her hatred of her mother and adoration of her father are part of the "debased familial affections" to which she falls victim and which "increased his pity" for her (190–91). In contrast, Anna's love for her mother is comparable to Lawrence's feelings for his own. There is nothing pathological about it. It is as pure as Anna's skin is unblemished. When Anna's nakedness evokes a Degas masterpiece to Lawrence, she could not be more unlike his wife, who increasingly comes to inspire his "shame" and "impatience" (193).

If, as the narrative progresses, the protagonist comes across as a more attractive figure than at the start of the novel, this cannot be said of the other characters. Lawrence, by his own admission, proves to be weak-willed and cowardly. The best reason he can think of for remaining with Vickie is that her lack of shame means that he "did not fear her judgement" (190). The implication is that he would have something to fear with Anna as his wife. She might see, as she does at this dinner, "that he is weak and that she is strong."[4]

The Hallidays' sex life is described at length but nonetheless remains somewhat elusive. This may be because the language Brookner employs in this instance is flat and uninspiring. But then, from Lawrence's standpoint so is life with Vickie. So Brookner might be forgiven the tabloid press phrasing of passages such as

"Sex with Vickie was violent, uninhibited: she was a conscientious and eager lover, thought out enticing scenarios, to which he always responded. . . . [H]e knew that while he despised the games he played with his wife he was now their victim" (193). The conciseness with which Brookner conveys the duplicity of Marie-Frances's fiancé is far superior. Being shown out the door, Anna feels that "the hand which he had placed in the small of her back slipped lower" (170).

Brookner works best as a miniaturist, with sexual appetites revealed over a soup tureen instead of in the larger canvas of a bedroom. Here, the dinner scene at the end of chapter 16 is a match for the custard-eating scene in all its horror at the end of *Look at Me:* "Gusts of fishy heat rose from the soup bowl which was lowered before her. The tiny jaws of mussels gaped from its crimson depths. Anna looked down in consternation. Courage was called for beyond the demands of politeness. Lawrence tucked a napkin into the neck of his cerulean shirt and set to with a pantomime of enthusiasm. The chunks of white fish which occasionally bobbled to the surface were not quite cooked through" (236–37). Comparable to her cooking, Vickie's sexuality is abundant but distinctly unsavory. Furthermore, as the word "pantomime" suggests, some of Lawrence's responsiveness may be put on for show.

Later, when Lawrence is not even allowed to leave their car to walk Anna to her door, the image of his subservience and entrapment is complete. In contrast, Anna is free to walk away both figuratively and literally. This foreshadows the final image of Anna walking away from Mrs. Marsh's daughter Philippa, the last reminder of her life in London. Having advised her to get out of her affair if it is not making her happy, Anna leaves the table where Philippa's unsatisfactory lover comes to sit. Anna is then described with a series of active verbs that tell as much about the way she now lives as how she crosses Paris streets. She is shown "plunging" into the traffic, and "holding" back the cars with her hand "to ward them off" (262). In total, what is conveyed is the control the protagonist at last has over her life. That her transformation is magnificent is captured in the image of her bringing Paris at the height of rush hour to a halt and the drivers' taking it "in good part" (262).

Previously a model of filial duty and self-sacrifice, Anna is now a model of emancipation, which Philippa literally follows "out into the bright, dark, dangerous and infinitely welcoming street" (262). Like happy endings, excessive use of adjectives is a rarity in Brookner's writing. Yet each adjective is crucial. The juxtaposition of "bright" with "dark" and "dangerous" with "infinitely welcoming" brings to mind a similar arrangement of seemingly contradictory messages in Dickens's *A Tale of Two Cities,* which opens, "It was the best of times, it was the worst of times, it was the age of wisdom, it was the age of foolishness, it was the epoch of belief, it was the epoch of incredulity, it was the season of Light, it was the season of Darkness. . . ."[5] Implicit in both passages is that these are eventful times. The image of Anna going out into a street symbolizes the start of a new life, one that bears a striking resemblance to the final words of *Little Dorrit,* except that Dickens sends his protagonist off with a husband "into the roaring streets."[6]

The full impact of the images at the end of *Fraud* comes from their contrast to what came previously. Although this is a novel about "starting over," most of the text concerns events preceding its onset, or ones that seemingly veer off into other directions. Yet the impact of the last scene would be infinitely less without a knowledge of who the elegantly dressed woman with the "slender back" stopping traffic is. The entire novel is effectively an assemblage of scenes that tells just that. The subject of Anna's identity is raised from the start, with the efforts of the police to build a character profile of her to the inability of those who are interviewed to fill in many details. Not since *Providence* has a protagonist received so much attention in this regard.

Yet for Anna, as for Kitty Maule, interest extends only so far. The irony of Lawrence's having been the one to set off a police investigation is that he previously had not given Anna much thought. Furthermore, the one time when he does genuinely show concern for her is when she least needs it. Unlike the protagonist of *Providence,* however, Anna is not portrayed as a victim. Whereas all of the secondary characters appear at first to be better off than the protagonist, on closer inspection the opposite is shown to be the case. The way in which the detective-style opening of the novel could suggest the discovery of a corpse as much as a living person foreshadows other mistaken deductions. In contrast to *Providence,* in which Kitty misinterprets the information at hand, in *Fraud* everyone but Anna fails to assemble the facts correctly.

As the final scene set in Paris confirms, Anna is not the poor virgin that Mrs. Marsh and others supposed her to be. Unlike Philippa's mother, Anna guesses that Philippa is having an affair and an ill-fated one. While her advice makes Philippa end it, this does not make her anything like the prig Blanche is in *The Misalliance.* More accurately, Anna emerges as a form of Biblical *wise* virgin, perhaps not waiting for the messiah, but with no less faith and "hope for a good outcome, a good cause" (261).

In retrospect, Brookner's names for the characters in *Fraud* reveal more that is true than false about them. Vickie is not half as regal as this diminutive for Victoria would suggest. Although she is the center of attention when Lawrence first meets her at a party, she has no more substance than the scant red dress she wears that night. Rather than aligning her with the grandeur and dignity associated with Queen Victoria, the name in its diminutive form suggest something not fully developed. Lawrence's opinion that even her sexual experimentation is "not grown up" confirms the implication that Vickie is childish (193). If she has not got the makings of a respected and beloved queen, then what does the future hold? Once Lawrence marries her, he learns. Neither lover nor wife, the words that are used to describe what Vickie is to Lawrence are "partner in vice" (193). If the name Vickie did not seem to fit this character, who bears so little resemblance to a queen, that is because it should more accurately be associated with the noun that it resembles: *vice*.

The protagonist's name also suggests a word that indicates her character. Said quickly, Anna Durrant, comes close to sounding like the noun "endurance." This would fit the image of her being long-suffering. But it also captures the essence of her spirit, which, unlike Lawrence's, is not downtrodden but long-lasting in the positive sense of being resilient, which is symbolized by the last image of her on a Paris street. In contrast, her mother never progresses to that point. She never recovers from the loss of either of the men in her life. Her inability to take control of her life is mirrored in the fact that she cannot even look after herself. More of a child than an adult in many ways, the name "Amy" points to a character who is diminutive in more than merely physical stature.

Two other names are more ironic than anything. The bigamist, George Ainsworth, turns out not to be *worth* Amy Durrant's love. And Lawrence's middle name is Merlin, the same as the magician from Arthurian legend. It is significant that Anna should be the one to ask what the initial "M" stands for, because she is also the only one to see past Lawrence's perfect demeanor, just as Merlin is by his female nemesis.

The fact that Lawrence is not quite what he seems is a motif in the text that is developed to the fullest extent in chapter 11. "The only son of a Leicester newsagent," Lawrence goes on to Cambridge University, where he obliterates all trace of his lower-middle-class northern English background (139). With his voice kept down, he impresses his patients with what appears to be his gentleness and deep concern for them. Yet he is actually concealing that he does not belong in the southeast of England any more than to the upper classes to which his wife and his patient Mrs. Marsh belong.

As with so much else associated with Lawrence, there are flaws in the new identity he constructs for himself. These are most glaring when he is with his upper-class wife. When Anna is at the Hallidays' for dinner, she witnesses the difference in their backgrounds when they clash on three trivial matters. The first is heating. Accustomed to a coal fire, Lawrence finds his house too warm. But when he lowers the thermostats on the radiators, Vickie turns them right up again with cries of "we'll freeze in here" (235). The second is drinking. Lawrence prefers beer but is forced by Vickie to have wine from her father's private cellar. In this instance, Vickie exposes Lawrence for being a fraud. As he is pouring out the wine, his wife tells Anna that her father has been "trying to train Lawrence's palate, without much success" (235). The third is food. Lawrence misses the food that is commonly associated with his original social class, such things as bacon sandwiches and fried eggs (233). Vickie's cooking is too exotic. Its "complicated smells" make him feel like a stranger in a foreign land (233).

Lawrence obviously functions as far more than a romantic interest in the narrative. As the dinner scene illustrates, his is a fraudulent life. Yet unlike those of George Ainsworth and Philippe Dunoyer, the compensations are few. Similarly, the contrast between the reasons for his faithfulness to Vickie and Anna's devotion to her mother could not be more striking. Although both Lawrence and Anna regard these relationships as imprisoning, the latter's is superior because it is based on strength not weakness. The message in *Fraud* is that starting over takes courage, but sometimes the meek are stronger than they seem.

Dolly

Always let them think of you as singing and dancing!
Dolly, 127

Known as *A Family Romance* in Britain, Brookner's next novel is called *Dolly* in the United States. Jane Manning is the protagonist and first-person narrator, but this is principally the story of Dolly, her aunt. If *Fraud*'s Anna seemed an unlikely character to become an inspiration for others, Dolly would appear to be an even remoter possibility. For one thing, there is initially no trace of affection or admiration from the standpoint of her niece. An uneasy relationship is suggested from the start, as the novel opens with the words, "I thought of her as the aunt rather than as my aunt" (1). Further on, she says "Dolly—the aunt—was a misfit. It was without surprise that I learned that Dolly was not her real name."[7] The reflective tone of the narrative is recognizable, so too is the subject of difficult female alliances. The opening pages of *Brief Lives* come to mind, even passages from *The Misalliance*. However, the word "misfit" introduces another dimension, one that aligns Dolly not only with Julia Wilberforce or Sally Beamish but also those protagonists like *Providence*'s Kitty Maule who are "difficult to place" (5).

Dolly's similarity to many of Brookner's protagonists is evident from a brief outline of her background. Dolly (whose real name is Marie-Jeanne) was born to German parents but is not German. Her mother was Catholic and her father Jewish but, like Ruth Weiss in *The Debut,* Dolly seems not to have been raised particularly as either. She lives in England but is French, not English. She is devoted to her mother who, like Kitty's grandmother who raises her in *Providence,* makes a living as a dressmaker. Never knowing her father and having to look after her mother before she herself is fully an adult, she is virtually an orphan. Like Fay in *Brief Lives,* she marries someone with a higher social standing than herself and is never wholly accepted by her mother-in-law. Her marriage is a disappointment but she remains with her husband until his death, just as Harriet does in *A Closed Eye*. In late middle age, she finds herself alone and having to construct a new identity for herself.

What makes *Dolly* much more than a loose weaving of various threads from previous novels is the particular slant that the first-person narrative by her niece gives to the text. The details of Dolly's life are told from Jane's perspective based on stories her mother told and her own memories of her aunt. This is not a sentimental journey. Yet the sense of wonder in the child's perspective invests Dolly with a magnificence from the start. "I had an impression of blackness and of whiteness: black eyes and white teeth," recalls Jane of her first meeting with her aunt (6). The image of Dolly would be frightening if supported by any words or acts of cruelty on her part. Lacking these, Dolly comes across most of all as a unique and imposing presence, one that is maintained throughout the narrative. As for any animosity she stirs in Jane, this seems to be more the result of a child's naturally simplistic view of the world in which people are good or evil and everything is perceived in clear-cut, "black and white" terms.

Jane's inability to understand the complexities of Dolly's relationship with her mother, Henrietta Manning, foreshadows her own relationship with her aunt. Returning to her first impression of her aunt, two features stand out. Dolly is perceived as being an unsettling presence ("I resented Dolly even then for invading my parents' peaceful world") and inscrutable ("She did not fondle me or take me on her lap, as I smugly expected her to do, but simply smiled those vivid and meaningless smiles at me and adjured me, in a heightened voice, to be a good girl and not to upset my mother") (6). The child's perspective invites parallels between Dolly, with her disturbing toothy smile, and the Cheshire cat, with the same, in Lewis Carroll's *Alice's Adventures in Wonderland* (1865). Another aspect of this is what she tells Jane: "Let them think of you as always singing and dancing" (6). This advice makes no more sense to the child, "four, or possibly five" years old, than do the Cheshire cat's words when Alice asks which way she ought to go. "That depends a good deal on where you want to get to," he answers (ch. 6). Dolly is similarly presented as a figure who guides Jane on her way through life, but the wisdom of whose words appear at first to be nonsensical.

This is where *Dolly* becomes the account of a very different female relationship from that in either *Brief Lives* or *The Misalliance*.

STARTING OVER

In *Brief Lives,* Fay is younger yet more knowing than Julia, who is not even aware that her husband has cheated on her for years with this friend. In *The Misalliance,* the child, Nellie, knows innately more about love than the novel's middle-aged protagonist. In contrast, the protagonist in *Dolly* is younger than her counterpart *and* less wise. Another difference is that Jane has virtually no life of any consequence beyond that in which Dolly is directly involved. As a result of the protagonist's youth and the focus in the narrative on the events of Dolly's life, Jane is a far less developed character, her role being essentially that of an observer. Yet unlike Anna Durrant, who in *Fraud* is a witness to and perpetrator of a fraud (in the form of her cheerfulness while caring for her mother), there are no such parallels between Jane and Dolly, least of all any in which Jane emerges as morally superior. This feature of her character does not make her a negative figure; rather, Jane comes across as someone on the brink of life beginning. In this respect, Jane is comparable to Dolly. For although the latter may be a generation older, she is repeatedly shown as having to start her life again. The first instance of this recounted in the narrative is when Dolly's husband Hugo dies. This is part of a chronicle of upheavals in Dolly's life that form a pattern of loss and survival. In the end, Dolly is an inspiring figure nonetheless for being hard to like.

In another contrast to the lives of Julia in *Brief Lives* and Sally in *The Misalliance,* the events in Dolly's life are larger and potentially more devastating than in either of these two. Whether by chance or will, the fact that Dolly escapes the gravest consequences makes her a model of resilience on a scale as great as the events themselves. As is characteristic in Brookner's writing, however, even monumental events are not dramatized.

The first of these is her husband's death, which is preceded by a description of Dolly in a doorway about to leave Jane's house for a bridge party. "Always make a good impression," she tells Jane before she goes, another version of her standard advice about singing and dancing (23). Then Jane recounts her transformation "into a glamorous and pretty woman," which points to more than mere physical beauty (23). Here, though only a child, Jane observes what in Dolly's character sets her apart from her mother and herself: "an excitement, a girlishness . . . as if in the course of that evening, or of the next, or of the one after that, some event might occur, some meeting, some transforming circumstance, that might just change her life for ever" (23). The next paragraph, in its entirety, reads "The next thing we heard was that Hugo had died, suddenly and unexpectedly" (23).

The loss of a husband is irreparably damaging to women in Brookner's novels. Kitty's mother, Marie-Therese, who is widowed in her early twenties in *Providence,* sets the standard for devastated widows. Yet even those who appear less traumatized, such as the protagonist's mother in *Lewis Percy,* say little and do even less until their deaths. Although in *Brief Lives,* the widowed Fay is presented more positively, even this is in the shadows of her own mother's decline. Since so many of these devastated widows are mothers (in some cases mothers-in-law) of Brookner's protagonists who have a strong sense of filial duty, their half-lived lives affect more than themselves. They contribute to the image that families are both practically and emotionally burdensome.

Dolly's widowhood is different. Although both Henrietta and Dolly enter into "raucous sobs of uncensored grief" over Hugo's death, Dolly recovers more immediately afterwards. The image of Dolly putting away her handkerchief symbolizes the end of her grieving. Moving from a tone of matter-of-factness to pride that the funeral was so "beautifully" conducted and well attended, Dolly's recovery is foreshadowed in this scene (26). Writing that "although the eyes were sad and lost the thin lips were resolute," Brookner makes the point that the change in Dolly is an act of will and not evidence of her lack of feeling (27). This view is emphasized by her farewell to the Mannings: "I'm not one to feel sorry for myself. If I have to put on an act I'll put on an act. Singing and dancing: that's what it's all about" (27). She says these words while rising from a chair, a movement that is more significant than it might at first appear. It sets her apart from other Brookner widows who remain in chairs or beds with no will to move on.

When Henrietta reflects afterwards that Dolly is "quite remarkable," the image of Dolly as an admirable and exceptional figure seems complete (29). What follows, however, is even more significant for dispelling any suggestion that Dolly might also be perceived as self-sacrificing and pitiful. Bluntly asking "How much?" Paul Manning raises the subject of money that will surface time and again in relation to Dolly (29). For, unlike the quintessential Brookner protagonist, Dolly has substantial worries in this area. With no legacy of her own, no education and no job, Dolly is wholly dependent on charity from her in-laws. Yet, in contrast to Brookner's other devastated widows, she is not portrayed as pitiful.

One way in which Brookner conveys this character's vitality is in the movement always associated with her. Rarely in one place for long, she is repeatedly shown entering or exiting from rooms, houses, cars, etc. References are made to her journeys to and from Belgium. Like the advice that becomes her hallmark, Dolly is repeatedly shown on dance floors and in the silk dresses that give the impression that she is dancing even when she is not. In contrast, the Mannings are presented as stagnant. Seated in their living room, reading silently to themselves or off to bed early, the tempo never quickens except when Dolly appears. Then, even Henrietta comes to life as she contemplates which restaurant to take her to and what she should wear. When her husband afterwards bemoans the expense, it is hard to thwart the impulse to shout, "Live a little!" For although we are led by Jane to understand that the Mannings are a loving family, their lives seem meager in comparison to Dolly's, which is devoid of love but rich in experience that extends well beyond the interior of an English suburban living room.

World events are rarely mentioned in Brookner's novels. *Latecomers* is the notable exception, but even there the adult Hartman and Fibich are removed from the Holocaust by a safe distance of miles and years. Although in *Family and Friends* Sofka's son Frederick spends the duration of the World War II in Italy, it is described as "a time of astonishing calm, even happiness" (138). An astonished reviewer for the *Jewish Chronicle* asks, "Are we really expected to believe the Jewish Frederick runs a hotel in Italy during the war, without a single tremor of fear or foreboding."[8] The same criticism is raised with regards to *Dolly:* "Not one German officer banging at the door? Really?"[9] Brookner shows a refusal to dramatize events here as elsewhere. "All was peace and amity at the Hotel Windsor in Brodighera" not because the war did not touch Frederick, but because his wine cellar was stocked well enough to please the palates of the German officers for the duration (139). Dolly and her mother are also effectively collaborators. By keeping the Paris prostitutes in the latest fashion, Dolly and her mother not only do "quite well under the Occupation," they also earn "the protection of a street network of girls, many of whom had joined up with German officers," but not without concealing their German origins before the Occupation and their Jewishness afterward (62). Just as Frederick in *Family and Friends* remains "a happy playboy . . . in spite of the war and the scarcely alluded-to Holocaust," Dolly retains her trust in a better future around the corner.[10]

For Dolly, the war years are an education in survival that Brookner depicts as being part chance and part resilience. Worthiness is not a factor. A will to live is what matters. In this respect, Dolly provides an altogether different model of womanhood than Henrietta does for Jane. Brookner conveys this in their different physique, dress, speech, and manner. Besides being more in every way (more fleshy, luxurious, animated, and vibrant), Dolly has an aptitude for changing herself that Jane's mother does not exhibit. Just as during the war she *stopped* being German or Jewish, Dolly adjusts herself to fit each new situation and environment in her life to come.

If Dolly is chameleon-like, Jane's mother is more like the last in a species on the verge of extinction. How differently these two women live after their husbands' deaths illuminates the difference in how they have lived their lives. Whereas Dolly becomes even more animated, Henrietta becomes quieter and more passive than ever before. Dolly goes out. Henrietta stays in. Dolly embarks on an affair. Henrietta watches television serials or soap operas all day. Dolly finds a social circle, makes friends, and entertains. Henrietta becomes a recluse, confused by illness into thinking her daughter is her dead husband. These scenes in which Henrietta's mental deterioration matches the physical damage to her heart are not dramatized but recounted by Jane in a few words. One such incident is related in a single sentence: "When I got up to go, picking up some vague approximation of a briefcase, she got up with a smile on her face and kissed me, for all the world as if I were my father and she were seeing me off to work" (135).

As suits the quintessential image of the wandering Jew, Dolly makes numerous moves, seeming to be constantly in motion as she goes from Germany to France, Belgium, then England (including return visits to Belgium), and from staying at one address to staying at another and another in the London area. This might amount to a negative image were it not for the parallel story of Henrietta's life, which Jane also recounts. The resulting juxtaposition of Dolly's wanderings with Henrietta's atrophy makes the former anything but negative. Particularly since Henrietta's immobility is symptomatic of the heart disease that kills her, Dolly's mobility becomes equated with life.

In chapter 3, Jane describes Dolly's first meeting with Hugo in terms of that innate propensity for survival that sets her aunt apart from the protagonist's mother. Exhibiting a deftness on the dance floor, which is matched by an adeptness at learning other languages, Dolly impresses Toni Ferber, who does not see beyond her charm to realize that she is a penniless immigrant to England. Fooled in part by the stylish evening dress that Dolly is wearing and Dolly's reference to her mother as "a well-known dressmaker in Paris" (the inference being that she is a haute couture designer on par with Chanel), Toni believes Dolly to be "a replica of herself" (70). Hugo "might marry her, she thought. She saw no difficulty in persuading him to do so, she who had held his hand until he was eleven years of age" (71). As the last sentence implies, women are substantially more powerful than men in this novel. Dolly naturally takes over where Toni leaves off in dominating Hugo. Even Paul Manning is powerless to dissuade Henrietta from giving Dolly regular gifts of money. As for Dolly's lover Harry, he is an exception. A manipulator of women, he is also set apart from the other male characters in the novel because of his working-class, East End background.

Brookner rarely ventures beyond the milieu of the middle classes, except possibly to move up the social ladder, as she does, for example, in *Providence* and *Look at Me*. Even the protagonists of *Brief Lives* and *Lewis Percy,* who come from lower social classes, move on. Apart from brief flashbacks to their earlier lives, those novels have as their focus the same middle-class world as all of Brookner's novels. *Dolly* is no exception. Described as being "socially not quite what they were used to," Harry is designated an outsider. In this regard, he and Dolly are alike. More than Dolly's foreignness, her lack of a husband is cited as the reason for her lack of status. With Harry at her side, her position is altered for the better in spite of his being working-class. The reason for this is his sexuality, which makes the other women's husbands look moribund indeed according to Jane, who likens him to "the sexual equivalent of an osteopath or a chiropractor: he offered 'relief,' and gave, as he thought, satisfaction all around" (212–13). Brookner's wit in passages such as this also offers relief from the downward turn of events in Dolly's later years. Slighted by family members who leave her a pittance or nothing in their wills, Dolly advances into old age with fewer resources than ever. What is more, Jane alone is privy to her aunt's heartbreak when Harry absconds with her money. The scenario is reminiscent of Ainsworth's treatment of Amy Durrant in *Fraud,* as is the fact that events are presented from the perspective of a daughter figure in both texts. Yet the same experience does not predetermine the same end. Dolly is altered but not destroyed by her experience.

In keeping with the pattern throughout her life, Dolly adjusts herself to a new role, which is something that Anna's mother in *Fraud* could never do. Having lost her social circle when Harry leaves her, Dolly seeks out another, this time of widowed and single older women. She swaps her imported silk dresses for British department store clothing and, as Jane observes, anyone "meeting her now for the first time would simply register her as an elderly person, for this was her new card of identity, the one she proffered when she went to afternoon performances at the cinema" (246).

Jane also shows an ability to start again or to become someone new. Following the death of both her parents, she writes a book on the subject for children, which launches her on a writing career that brings her international fame. In the final chapter of *Dolly,* Jane recounts her "last visit to America" (249). A shift in focus from Dolly to Jane's own life occurs earlier in the novel but to altogether different ends. When Jane takes a job in a press cutting agency (literally cutting items out of newspapers) it is in order to escape from the depressing figure of her mother at home. The fact that a job as dreary as this is the highlight of a seventeen-year-old's life points to two things: first, the extent to which her mother's decline has affected her; second, how much Jane is like her mother in being content with so little.

Jane is still recognizable at the conclusion of *Dolly.* An astute observer of human behavior, she sees the vocal young feminists at women's colleges in America as rather shallow, more intent on reaffirming a preconceived view of the world than actually hearing her answers to their questions. The academic women in their fifties who were "long divorced or else widowed" impress her more with their quiet dignity (249). Still not one to be confrontational, Jane's views are conveyed less through dialogue than reflection. Her compatibility with the older female professors further contributes to an image of her superiority.

The fact that Jane is the guest speaker on these American campuses naturally makes her the focus of attention, although she herself continues to be an observer. This lends her a star quality that is totally in contrast to previous images and invites parallels between Jane and Dolly. Although not everyone likes Jane's views (no more than everyone likes those of her aunt), she has a stature that her mother does not. In the end, Jane exhibits a strength of character that does not falter before her American audiences any more than Dolly's ever did before her bridge-playing friends. As Jonathan Yardley writes in the *Washington Post,* for Jane to start this new life "takes real courage. But after all else is said and done, courage is what Dolly—the novel and the person alike—is all about."[11]

A Private View

Now was the moment to take stock.
                                    A Private View, 3

More immediately than in either *Fraud* or *Dolly, A Private View* (1994) begins with a death. The opening paragraph tells of the death of the protagonist's friend who "had inconveniently succumbed to cancer just when they were enabled, by process of evolution, or by that of virtue rewarded, more prosaically by the fact of their simultaneous retirement, to take their ease, to explore the world together, as had been their intention."[12] As the word "inconveniently" implies, Putnam's death is presented entirely in terms of how it has an impact on the protagonist's life. Yet the repeated use of "they" in the sentences that follow suggests a connection between these two characters beyond that which the image of mere traveling companions or the word "inconveniently" might convey. The length of the sentences and their complexity makes for a decidedly slow start to this novel, as befits the state of the protagonist who "felt half dead himself" after his friend's death (5). Putnam's death has done more than made George Bland rethink his travel plans. It has thrust him into reflecting on his entire life. Note, however, that it is life, not death, which occupies the protagonist's thoughts. The finality of death is absolute and uncushioned by visions of an afterlife. As is characteristic of Brookner's depiction of death, her protagonists have no religious faith that might provide solace or comfort.

Initially, the image of Putnam as a traveling companion may not seem to warrant the significance that Bland attaches to him. In addition, Bland's distress over the alteration to his travel plans that Putnam's death necessitates should make him appear petty indeed. Yet this is Brookner's understatement at work. For Putnam is Bland's traveling companion in more than a literal sense. Metaphorically, he and Bland have journeyed together for the better portion of their lives, from their modest beginnings in the same company to their success and retirement. This much is clear from the first chapter; so too is the irony that the first actual journey that they plan should not occur.

Ironies abound in *A Private View*. Retirement, which Bland envisaged as a period in which he and his friend would be together, marks their point of separation. Rather than being a new beginning, Putnam's death makes this a time in which things end. Bland finds himself in a state of reflection instead of activity. Looking back instead of forward, regret, not satisfaction, is the emotion that grips him.

STARTING OVER

Inevitably, putting off their trip together until after retirement comes to symbolize a life of deferred pleasure for Bland.

The contrast could not be greater between "that long journey to the Far East, by the slowest route possible" that Bland had looked forward to with Putnam, and his solitary stay in Nice, from which he returns home early after only four days (11). The first destination epitomizes the yearning for adventure that these men feel. Employing the words "Far East" instead of specifying say Japan or Thailand suggests a journey to uncharted lands with uncommon experiences compatible with their fantasy "to explore the world together" (4). No such exoticism is attached to France, let alone Nice, which is described mundanely enough as "a town" (3).

A dining room is the setting for the first in a number of pivotal moments for the protagonist. While sitting in an expensive restaurant, Bland sees Putnam beside him. His friend is not eating heartily but "clutching the latest of a series of Get Well cards" (4). Although it is clear that this is Bland's involuntary memory at work, reducing the scene to Putnam's "skeletal hand" and silence makes this as disturbing as a spectral visitation (4). The fact that Bland has for years dined out with Putnam contributes to this impression. Memory is something that haunts and disturbs. No pleasure can be taken without Putnam's absence being remembered. Moreover, his friend comes to represent the folly of self-denial. Putnam cannot take his wealth with him, and Bland cannot even remotely enjoy it without feeling shame that his friend's loss is his own gain and one that brings him no satisfaction.

Retirement and bereavement are the focus at the start of the novel. But from the middle of the second chapter, when Katy Gibb appears in the text, Bland is moved to speak and act. If *A Private*

View comes to life at this point it is a direct result of the protagonist's being jolted from his reveries. The present, not the past, is suddenly more significant. Whereas the first chapter is made up of
flashbacks and introspective passages, the next contains dialogue
and scenes in which Bland is called upon to do something now. As
with all of Brookner's protagonists, Bland's actions tend to be in
response to events as opposed to initiating them. Nonetheless, there
is a marked contrast between the virtually static opening of the novel
and the pages that follow.

This transformation begins in a small way. A telephone rings.
Astonished and alarmed, Bland's reaction completes a picture of a
solitary and quiet life. With Putnam dead and his affairs settled,
there is only one person Bland can imagine might call him. This is
Louise, with whom Bland had been in love when he was young. The
story of their failed romance is recounted in chapter 1. A lack of
nerve, not love, on Bland's part results in his losing Louise to
another man. Now a widow in her sixties, she calls Bland every Sunday and meets him when she is in town. Beyond her, there is no one
in his life who is not paid to be there. The exchange of money with the
apartment doorman and his cleaning woman highlights this reality.

When the voice at the end of the telephone turns out not to be
Louise, Bland is relieved. The inference is that Louise would not
call other than on a Sunday unless there were something terribly
wrong. Orderliness characterizes Bland's life, just as it does the
decor of his home. When Katy suggests moving a writing desk, he
resolutely says no. Yet he will look upon the arrangement of his
rooms with less satisfaction later on, when Katy is about to leave.
Returning to his empty apartment, he is struck by how much his
"sitting-room, as Putnam had once observed, looked like the waiting-

room of a Harley Street psychiatrist, except that would be warmer, with an even purring warmth designed to allay disquiet" (212). Harley Street is the address in London of some of the most expensive and fashionable private doctors' offices in Britain. What is negative about this image, however, is the correlation made between a waiting room and a "sitting-room," or living room. The implication is that Bland's rooms reflect his life, which has largely been spent waiting rather than living. The implication of the reference to psychiatrists' offices is that Bland's way of life is an unhealthy aberration. Serving as a microcosm for Bland's world, his apartment mirrors the primacy he has put on order and control at the cost of comfort and pleasure.

Bland's antithesis is Katy Gibb, whose life is similarly captured by an interior. On the morning after she leaves for America, Bland surveys his neighbors' apartment in which she had been living. The contrast between his own living space and that which she appropriated could not be more striking. Not only is it a mess, but all appearances are that she is still living in it. Although the "air vibrated with her absence," it also is permeated with her presence (226). From the television having been left on and ironing board and iron left out to the dented pillow where she had slept, signs of Katy's stay are everywhere. Were this her own apartment, the contrast to Bland's would be symbolic enough of their different concepts of comfort. The fact that Katy is a squatter who has fooled Bland into handing over his neighbors' keys, makes the disarray she leaves behind all the more significant. This is not lost on Bland, who cannot help but admire "her incredible insouciance" (226).

Whereas the image of Maurice with his hand on the small of Miss Fairchild's back is a horrible one for Kitty that makes the end of *Providence* so startling, the truth about Katy is not destructive, but the reverse, for Bland. For one thing, he admires her resilience, likening her to the mythological phoenix that rises from the ashes. For another, "the wreckage that she left behind" can be set right by his cleaning woman (227). Words conveying Bland's admiration for Katy feature so much in this final chapter that anything short of positive emotions are difficult to attach to him. Bland's image of himself as the survivor of a shipwreck dispels any suggestion that Katy has destroyed his life, although the implication is that her presence is akin to a raging sea or storm. In fact, the images that Bland attaches to Katy bring to mind the adventures that might be associated with the Far East travels that he dreamed of with Putnam. In this regard, the novel comes full circle back to the beginning.

The difference is that Bland now knows that change cannot be had as readily as a plane ticket. One trip with Putnam, however eventful, would not make him a new man any more than it could undo the years of staidness preceding it. At best, meeting Katy makes him dream again of journeys both literal and metaphorical. Although the trip to Rome with Katy never materializes, the fact that Bland conceives of it at all *and* has the courage to ask her is proof of the change in him. Like his name, and as his uneventful past illustrates, the protagonist is bland or dull. Significantly, Katy is the only one to call him George, as if in her presence he is freed from his namesake. His actions compound this view. Whether he is drinking champagne or tea while Katy lounges in various states of undress beside him, there is nothing dull about Bland or these scenes.

What lends dramatic tension to every encounter between Bland and Katy is that Bland is enthralled by her. It also becomes increasingly apparent that Katy is after Bland's money. Given Bland's feelings of desire, the repeated image of Katy with streaming wet hair does not suggest slovenliness (in contrast to Louise's impeccable dress), but Aphrodite rising from the sea. Whether resembling a Greek goddess of beauty and fertility or an Egyptian and medieval symbol of everlasting life, Katy is anything but ordinary. This is what Bland comes to conclude. In comparison, he and Putnam, like Louise and his upstairs neighbor Mrs. Lydiard, are boringly respectable. Even their dependability is more a matter of habit than evidence of moral character.

By the end of *A Private View,* it is evident that Bland's lassitude after Putnam's death arises less from grief for his friend than for himself. The absence of companionship, compounded by the absence of work, reveals the barrenness of his life. It is significant that on the night when Katy leaves, Bland recalls speaking to Putnam on just this subject. "Why should life seem exciting only if there is the possibility of throwing it away?" he asks (223). Dismissed by Putnam as a romantic, Bland is revealed to be less like his friend than at first seemed the case. Although neither Putnam nor Bland exhibits any daring in his lifetime, the latter regrets this state of affairs. For this reason, Bland more closely resembles those protagonists of Brookner's who wish for more than their lives bring to them.

Given the entrapment Bland feels in his apartment, in old age and in retirement, images of flight or escape serve to reinforce this view by their failure to materialize. Thus, the novel begins with reference to the Far East trip that comes to symbolize lost chances. It concludes, however, with Bland inviting Louise on a cruise. The telephone rings routinely, as ever, with Louise updating Bland on the inconsequential events of her week when he asks her. The fact that the text ends without an answer, or that Katy refused an earlier invitation, or that Brookner's protagonists often have their plans thwarted (in *The Debut* and *The Misalliance* for example) does not wholly diminish the optimism of this scene. One reason is that Louise is presented as a far more accessible object of desire than Katy. The other is that there is genuine affection and compatibility between Bland and Louise. Given his regret for losing her once before through inaction, second chances might just this once be given to a Brookner protagonist

CHAPTER SIX

Journeying to the End

Incidents in the Rue Laugier,
Altered States, and *Visitors*

Incidents in the Rue Laugier

Any notation, any record, is better than none.
Incidents in the Rue Laugier, 233

The next three novels that Brookner wrote in the 1990s have many of the features of earlier ones, but also share a common new theme. Although vastly different from one another in terms of their protagonists, settings, and actions, each of them depicts a journey. In *Incidents in the Rue Laugier* (1995) this takes the form of a daughter's search for her mother. In *Altered States* (1996) a man obsessively pursues a woman he loves. In *Visitors* (1997) a elderly woman embarks on the final stages of her life.

The first of these begins with a device reminiscent of the start of *Family and Friends,* except that in place of a family photograph, this time Brookner employs a notebook. The narrator is similarly in the dark as to its meaning. Yet more obviously than in *Family and Friends,* the text is pointed to as a construction of reality based more on imagination than fact. The fiction that accounts for all but the first and last chapters of *Incidents in the Rue Laugier* is based on the scant citations in an old notebook. This belonged to the narrator's mother, who is no longer alive to explain its significance. The implication from the start of the novel, however, is that even if she were still alive her daughter would be none the wiser, as there is little in the way of communication between them.

Maffy's knowledge of her mother is summed up in the words of the novel's opening sentence: "My mother read a lot, sighed a lot, and went to bed early."[1] Of these things she is certain. But their meaning eludes her. Ironically, it is with her mother's death that a route to further knowledge opens up. This is offered by a pink kimono and a notebook, neither of which she had ever seen before, the sole possessions of her mother's that she keeps. The kimono offers no obvious clues, not even that which a tag or monogram or even a stain might provide. Yet, its existence alone is suggestive enough on several counts. First, the sensuality suggested by its silk fabric, pink color, and exotic design seem wholly incompatible with the modest woman whom this protagonist knew. The implication is that there is another side to this woman that has been hidden away much as this article of clothing has been. Second, its foreignness hints at something beyond England and the English life that marriage made "Maude Gonthier, from Dijon," adopt (3). Third, and most important, its existence lends an aspect of mystery to its owner, which inspires Maffy to create the fiction that comprises the subsequent fourteen chapters. As an image, the significance of which goes unexplained until much later in the narrative, it also lends interest to this character who will be the focus of the novel.

Like the mother, the notebook is not English but French. Otherwise it is quite ordinary, as indeed this mother appears to be to her daughter. Comparable to the kimono, the content of this notebook is puzzling because the daughter cannot connect it to the mother she knew. The narrative that follows is an effort to make connections that would reveal the significance of each entry. Implicit in Maffy's endeavor is a belief in order and cause and effect. As is characteristic of Brookner's protagonists, she has faith in little else. Yet hers is not an embittered voice so much as a rational one. How precisely one event leads to another with no master plan in sight is the scheme of the narrative that follows. It is in this spirit that the story of Maude's life is told.

Typically, there is no sentimentalizing of parents in Brookner's novels. Nonetheless, the loss of a parent has considerable impact on the lives of her protagonists. *Incidents in the Rue Laugier* exemplifies this by its very premise. Apart from the first and last chapters, it is set entirely in a fictional past that Maffy reconstructs in order to live in the present. As Maffy explains at the close of the novel, her search for "those hidden lives" is a restorative, but limited, exercise (233). "A desire to bring my dead back to life," she says, made her link together the words in her mother's notebook (233). Yet there is never the suggestion that any truth is arrived at. In fact, Maffy concludes by saying that the meanings of some of the notebook citations still elude her. *Dames Blanches* is "particularly baffling" (233). It might refer to a street, a convent, a comic opera, or an ice cream. The effect of Maffy's ruminations is not to detract from the narrative that precedes them but to draw attention to the role of the writer. What limits the multiplicity of possible meanings is the arrangement in which a word finds itself. Writing is very much presented here by Brookner as a matter of ordering language. Since words have no intrinsic meaning, a literary text should be judged on its arrangement of language, not the rendering of any reality. Given the extent to which critics have remarked (often negatively) upon what they consider to be the autobiographical basis for Brookner's novels, particularly those featuring female protagonists, this could be taken as a reminder that writing is a craft. Many of Brookner's protagonists may lack artifice, but this is not to say that their author does.

Brookner draws attention to the imaginative dimension of any work of fiction in the initial pages of *Incidents in the Rue Laugier*. The first chapter, which serves as a preface to the story of Maud Gonthier, ends with these words: "It is a fabrication, one of those by which each of us lives, and as such an enormity, nothing to do with the truth. But perhaps the truth we tell ourselves is worth any number of facts, verifiable or not. This unrecorded story—unrecorded for a very good reason—is a gesture only, a gesture towards my mother, whom I have come to resemble, and who told me nothing either of what had happened, or what had failed to happen, and how she came to live with us, so far from home" (7). Calling the pages that follow a "fabrication" fits a pattern in which its content is referred to as "speculation" and its narrator as "unreliable" (6, 4). The implication is that readers *rely* on narrators not only to tell a story but also to tell it truthfully. This raises the epistemological question "What is truth?" Maffy offers an answer in the closing words of the novel, thereby suggesting that the act of writing is a journey to knowledge. What is true, she concludes, is "that most lives are incomplete, that death precludes explanation" (233). Although she is no closer to knowing her mother, she has learned this much from her efforts. All of Brookner's protagonists are wiser for their experiences by the end of her novels. But the similarity to Blanche in *The Misalliance* is strongest because knowledge is not so much registered and responded to emotionally. As in the tortuous final scene in *Providence*, it is reflected upon with an almost philosophical detachment.

A circular pattern of returning to the start of the text through words or images is a frequent feature of Brookner's novels. Yet the undermining of narrational authority in the first and last chapters of *Incidents in the Rue Laugier* sets it apart from the rest. This narrator's pleas *not* to be trusted ironically have the same effect as the refrain, "I'm telling you stories. Trust me" in Jeannette Winterson's *The Passion* (1987).[2] They draw attention to the reader's dependency on a narrator, one that is akin to that which travelers have for a guide. The parallels between reading and journeying are fairly apparent. Although Brookner foregoes employing giantesses as Winterson does, elements of the unknown or unexplored pervade the first and last chapters, which frame the text within the text that makes up *Incidents in the Rue Laugier*. Whereas fantastic elements remind us that Winterson's is a created world only just based on historical fact, Brookner's narrator admits the extent to which the story of Maud Gonthier is an invention. The difference is that for the latter, even that which is presented as uninvented (the kimono, the notebook entrees) has no reality beyond the text. Nonetheless, they serve as markers along the way while we read Maffy's narrative.

What Maffy's mother leaves her are effectively the tools of a writer, an article of clothing and notes representing images and words. Like the facts the police gather in their search for Anna in *Fraud,* their meaning is dependent on how they are assembled. The "evidence" of Maud Gonthier's life is slim indeed, a fact that saddens Maffy (7). But the presence of her daughter is proof of this mother's *existence*. What is needed so that "nothing is lost" is an assemblage which would give them meaning—any meaning (233). While some might interpret the view that Brookner presents at the end of *Incidents in the Rue Laugier* as the influence of new historicism or poststructuralist narrative theory, the references to Proust in these key first and last chapters are more conclusive and more in keeping with the intertextual literary references that are a standard feature of novels.

More so than historians, writers are common enough in Brookner's novels. The protagonists of *Look at Me, Hotel du Lac,* and *Dolly* write short stories, romance novels, and children's books respectively. Writers of scholarly works, from dissertations to lectures and books, include the protagonists in *The Debut, Providence, Lewis Percy,* and *Fraud.* But the nearest equivalent to Maffy is Fibich in *Latecomers,* who leaves his son a family history he has written. Both return to the past for their inspiration, and it is inspiring indeed. Although the family that Fibich writes about is lost in the Holocaust, the point of his memoir is to tell his son "what a good life it has been" (247). A similar wording is used to convey the purpose of recounting the sad story of Maud Gonthier's life. "All life is good," its creator contends (232).

The similarity between Maffy in *Incidents in the Rue Laugier* and Fibich in *Latecomers* is more obvious than it may first appear. Although their experiences are vastly different, both are adult orphans who feel the need "to return" to the past to rediscover a parent or parents. They also regard themselves as witnesses to these parents' lives. However imperfectly they record events, their duty is to do just that. Filial duty is very much the subject of Brookner's novels, but in these texts it takes a form that links these children with historians. Both Maffy and Fibich assume this role out of dutifulness, but, moreover, because there is no one else to do so. Like Fibich, Maffy thinks of herself as a survivor. *Incidents in the Rue Laugier* concludes with her referring to "we, the survivors" or those like herself who are left "to explain" the inexplicable (233).

Parallels to the responsibility that many Jewish writers feel with regard to writing about the Holocaust come to mind. First, the experiences, though not their authors' own, are by inheritance their responsibility to record. Second, as Maffy says at the end of *Incidents in the*

Rue Laugier, "any notation, any record, is better than none" (233). Whether the form is documentary or fiction, the goal is remembrance. The third similarity concerns the yearning to explain or make sense of events. Maud Gonthier's sighs are a mystery to her daughter, who tries to give them meaning. From the former's reticence and the nature of the events which Maffy attaches to them, the difficulty of speech is understood to be relative to the difficulty of experiences. Silences and sighs make sense to Maffy only after she invents a tragic past for her mother.

All of Brookner's novels concern "coming of age," and most frequently in terms of their protagonists' marrying *or* failing to do so. In the worlds that the protagonists, particularly of her earlier novels, inhabit, marriage is depicted as a rite of passage. Whether it is idealized as an entry into English upper-class society, as it is by Kitty in *Providence,* or made a symbol for lost innocence when its reality shatters expectations, as it does in *Lewis Percy,* marrying is equated with maturity. These are the twin strains of the story Maffy constructs for her mother.

Maud Gonthier, like the protagonist of *Providence,* lacks belonging. Her French background is respectable, but her father's and grandfather's deaths leave her and her mother both marginalized and dependent on family. Tyler represents everything Maud is not: English, upper-class, and loved. The contrast between the reception given to these two houseguests at the summer home of Maud's aunt could not be greater, and epitomizes their respective places at the center or margins of society and happiness.

When Maud and Tyler come together it is no surprise. While Brookner's protagonists might be accused of being "dopey hangdog people," as one critic has put it, they have an uncommon knack nonetheless for attracting lovers.[3] Since everyone else is attracted to

Tyler, men and women alike, there is nothing exceptional about
Maud's falling in love with him. Like all of Brookner's male
enchanters, from Maurice in *Providence* to Nick in *Look at Me,* and
their female equivalents, Sally in *The Misalliance* to Katy in *A Private View,* Tyler is an object of fascination as much as love for
Maud. And comparable to these novels' protagonists (from Kitty to
Frances, Blanche, and George), she is as much a victim of her own
innocence as of Tyler himself.

After Tyler makes love to Maud then abandons her—a common
sequence in Brookner's novels, in which her protagonists have a
propensity for falling for "men who have 'cad' woven into their
hairpieces and rented sheets"—her mother says, "That is over now,
do you hear? You have the chance to be respectable again. Not every
woman is so lucky. You will settle down; we shall all settle down,
and be as we were" (133).[4] To Nadine Gonthier, "settle down"
means forget Tyler and marry his lackluster but well-meaning friend
Edward. Believing at first that she is pregnant, and afterwards bow-
ing to pressure from her mother, Maud goes to England as Edward's
wife but cannot erase the memory of her brief affair. A "sensation of
unreality" in which she cannot understand "how had it been possible to feel so much then, and so little now" pervades the rest of her
life (126). By inference, this accounts for the abstracted quality that
makes Maud so inaccessible to her daughter.

Those who finish Maffy's narrative "hoping she is wrong" are
missing the point.[5] Consider the alternative. Maud remains as elusive in death as during her life. Of course, this "tale of love and loss"
is merely a version of what might have been.[6] It is an imitation of
life as much as the maturity that Maud exhibits after losing Tyler is
a "simulacrum" (126). Yet it represents an effort to come to terms
with loss, to make sense of the inexplicable, and to make order of

seeming disorder. In these respects, the fiction that Maffy constructs is a passport for the future. Unreliable perhaps, if returning to the past were possible, it is nonetheless sufficient in that Maffy can look ahead once it is completed. Significantly, she does just this in the final pages of the novel. In a paragraph beginning, "I may sell the shop next year . . ." Maffy is looking ahead and thinking of herself for the first time (232)

The experience of writing her first novel (the only one that she says is autobiographical) made Brookner realize that self-analysis "leads nowhere—it is an art form in itself."[7] Similarly, Maffy's narrative is, as she admits, more form than substance. No closer to knowing her mother because of it, this could symbolize a journey without end. But the positive and forward-looking tone of the last chapter suggests otherwise. As a result, there is nothing pitiful or remotely pathological about Maffy's writing—in contrast, for example, to a Holocaust survivor's obsessive letter writing to her dead daughter in Cynthia Ozick's *The Shawl* (1980) or a young woman's fabrication that she is Anne Frank in Philip Roth's *The Ghost Writer* (1979). If parallels exist at all, they might be to Brookner herself, who sums up the cathartic effect of the creative act by saying, "Writing has freed me."[8]

Altered States

Find Sarah for me.

Altered States, 6

Actual physical journeys are basically of two kinds in Brookner's novels. The first kind embodies a new start, or hope of one, and Paris is the favored destination. The second involves a return to London and is, in comparison, a distinctly retrograde step. *Altered States* is an anomaly. It opens with a setting that promises a journey, but none transpires for its protagonist, who observes the trains but neither embarks nor disembarks from a single one. Alan Sherwood is no train watcher. He is an Englishman abroad who wants to buy an English newspaper. A delivery "usually arrived at about four o'clock," he says.[9] Whether the train is late or he is early is uncertain and passes into irrelevance because the protagonist's thoughts are elsewhere. A woman on the station platform has captured his attention. He wonders if she is Sarah.

In terms of the story that unfolds, newspapers are of no particular consequence. But as an image, the newspaper train could not hold more meaning. As the words "usually arrived" suggest, Alan has a faculty for observation in common with all of Brookner's protagonists. Untiring patience and a propensity to adopt routines are also evoked by these words and the image of him waiting on this platform. Given that Brookner's protagonists are usually polyglots, the bother to which he will go in order to acquire an English newspaper suggests more than a need for news. The implication is that he may be abroad but he is neither wholly immersed in the foreign culture nor distracted by it. England still has a hold on his thoughts just as Sarah has a hold on his heart.

Chapter 1 is made up almost entirely of this protagonist/narrator's introspections when he sees a woman who reminds him of her. The passion he felt for Sarah is intimated by the obsessiveness with which he ponders whether or not the woman on the platform could be she. Particularly revealing is that although her back is to him, he never tries to see her face. In a word, Alan Sherwood lacks boldness, which in Brookner's books means that he is doomed. For it is boldness, not virtue, according to Brookner, that brings good fortune to a person.[10] Happiness will as a result remain as elusive as Sarah is for him.

Even granting this protagonist's passive nature, his patience merely to ponder the back of the woman on the platform is significant. The positioning of him behind her mirrors his pursuit of Sarah. That the latter will remain just beyond his reach is suggested by the subsequent disappearance of the woman on the platform. The fact that he never sees her face is emblematic of how he never really knew Sarah. The contrast between his interest in the woman on the platform and her total unawareness of him also foreshadows his relationship with Sarah and his unrequited love for her. Most significantly, although he finally doubts that this woman is Sarah, the possibility remains. In this respect, not looking at her face may be a matter of choice. Ascertaining if this woman is Sarah would end his pursuit of her.

Altered States is not the story of a great love but of journeys without end. As illustrated in the opening chapter, the focus will be on the protagonist and his pursuit rather than the actual object of his desire, who remains as elusive as her name (she "might be Sarah Miller, or Sarah de Leuze") (4). The journeys in question are psychological rather than physical, a point that is made clear from the start of the novel, in spite of its railway setting and book jacket cover showing the same. Like Mrs. Miller, who pleads, "Find Sarah for me," the protagonist is ostensibly engaged in a quite tangible pursuit (8). In both cases, however, the focus in the narrative is less on the progress or failure of this endeavor than on the altering mental and emotional states "the pursuers" undergo.

While there is a similarity between Alan's yearning for "grand passions [that] are no longer the order of the day" and the striving

for romantic ideals of heroism in *Lewis Percy,* parallels between the
male protagonists of these texts go only so far. What makes *Altered
States* more than a reworking of Lewis Percy's failures is the way in
which Brookner parallels Alan's life with that of Mrs. Miller. In
contrast to Sarah, who is largely depicted as Alan's nemesis, Mrs.
Miller serves a mirror to further define Alan's character.

Like Sarah, Mrs. Miller is a somewhat elusive figure, at least
insomuch as "she has a strangely changing name and identity" (8).
But that is as far as the similarities go. Their name changes alone
reveal considerable differences. When Alan wonders if Sarah's last
name is Miller or de Leuze, his question is really whether or not she
has married. Mrs. Miller's name changes reveal considerably more
about her than merely her marital status. As the first words of chapter 3 suggest, this is because there *is* more substance to her. The
chapter begins in a recollection of the past: "I first encountered Jad-
wiga/Edwige" (23). On the very next page, this same character is
introduced to the protagonist as "Jenny" (25). Although Polish, she
has a French accent and considers herself "an English wife with an
English husband and an English family" (27). Three first names
(Jadwiga, Edwige, Jenny) and three national identities later (Polish,
French, English), the character that emerges is a highly resilient one
on a par with Brookner's Dolly. Like the latter, Jenny is physically
unimposing, but she is associated with both strength and endurance,
which her feet epitomize. The ugliness of them is the result of her
wearing a pair of shoes far too small for her feet when she was penniless in Paris. They were a gift from a lover. Neediness and suffering,
particularly in relation to a lover, are elements that invite comparison
between Jenny and Alan. Conversely, Sarah is associated with plenty.

The first time that Alan meets Jenny is, significantly, also the first time that he meets Sarah. Here, as in the initial image of the protagonist staring at a stranger whom he can only half see, the physical positioning of characters is highly significant. At Jenny's engagement party to Humphrey, Sarah is shown deliberately drawing attention (according to Alan) to the contrast between "herself, taut as a whipcord in her minute black suit and her low-cut silk shirt, and her uncle's elderly wife with her broken feet" (28). Observations of this kind recur throughout the narrative and make the protagonist's obsession with Sarah all the more difficult to understand. At no time is Alan's keen eye clouded by his feelings. The simple directness of statements such as "My name is Alan Sherwood and I am a solicitor, as were my father and grandfather before me" helps build a portrait of a sensible man not given to illusions (10). Yet he will obsess over someone who is quite obviously unworthy of him and unwilling to reciprocate these feelings.

The parallels between the protagonist's fate and that of Jenny are made increasingly apparent as the novel goes on. While both look to Sarah for love, similarities exist even before they meet her. The first intimation of this is when Allan and Jenny are initially described. Allan, who has been devoted to his widowed mother, suddenly finds himself dispensable when she remarries. Jenny has just married Humphrey and come to England for the first time. Both are figures of displacement. Some time later, when Allan's mother remarks that Jenny is a "poor darling" who "never really fitted in," the irony is that these words are just as applicable to her son (183). That she does not realize this contributes to a picture of the protagonist's private suffering and experience of alienation. The same thing occurs when his mother speaks of Jenny's "attitude to Sarah" and her fantasy "that the two of them would become close" (183).

The attempts that Alan and Jenny make to alter their situations (his feelings of abandonment by his mother, her lonely poverty in France after leaving Poland) are particularly revealing, and foreshadow more mistakes to come. Allan marries a friend of Sarah's named Angela after she cares for him when he has the flu. She makes a satisfactory enough mother substitute, but a disappointing wife. Jenny's marriage to an Englishman similarly provides material comfort but little else. Home, as the embodiment of unconditional love and acceptance, is somewhere else for both Allan and Jenny.

Paris, which held the promise of something better when Jenny met Humphrey, is also the setting for Alan's hopes. Yet his trip to Paris also ends in disaster. Reminiscent of Mimi's failed rendezvous with the dance instructor's son in *Family and Friends,* Alan waits all of one night in a Paris hotel for his love to come to him. Sarah never does. Just as Mimi's life is forever altered by her experience, Alan finds nothing the same and all for the worse as well. Called back to London with news that Angela has miscarried, events go from bad to worse. Severe depression ends with her suicide. Although Alan never met Sarah in Paris, his intention to do so makes him feel responsible for the succession of events that follow his one act of boldness. This is compounded by how others attribute responsibility to him either indirectly (as Humphrey and his friend Brian do) or directly (when Jenny says, "You were after Sarah, weren't you?") (150).

When Alan goes to Vif, a dull town in off-season, the implication is that he is sent there, much as Edith is in *Hotel du Lac* after she deserts her fiancé on their wedding day. Scandalous behavior that is wholly out of character for these protagonists is condemned as much as anything that can actually be credited with having direct consequences. Thus Alan, like Edith, regards this journey as a form of punishment. Significantly, Alan is shown in Vif at both the start and end of the novel, although this is decades after the original reason for his going there. The implication is that his punishment is never ending.

Alan Sherwood is arguably the least likable of any of Brookner's protagonists since Blanche in *The Misalliance*. Seemingly trivial details, such as his throwing out his wife's childhood teddy bear, contribute to a less than sympathetic picture of him. In his relations with Jenny, however, he is highly considerate, compassionate, and generous. When Sarah inherits the apartment in which Jenny is living, he convinces Sarah to hand it over to her. Never knowing the full part that Alan played in this transaction, Jenny believes that her dreams have come true. Her love for Sarah has been reciprocated at last. "I knew Sarah was fond of me," she tells Alan who allows her this fantasy (209). Although he thinks that he is "unlikely to bring her further joy," other fantasies will follow. The search for Sarah is the ultimate one.

Significantly, the novel ends with Alan anticipating the next time he will see Jenny, not Sarah. Although in chapter 1 he concludes that the woman on the train platform is not Sarah, he will tell Jenny that he is "definitely on Sarah's trail," having seen her in Vif (229). "The transformation of an unremarkable affair into a sort of pilgrimage has a certain nobility," he surmises (229). Alan's pursuit of Sarah in the past may have been folly, but it becomes an act truly of love in the end. Comparable to *Hotel du Lac,* in which its romance novelist defends rewriting the world as a fairer place, *Altered States* presents the case that fantasy as much as faith is essential to life.

Visitors

> There were no precedents for the journey ahead, yet
> it was felt to be hazardous.
>
> *Visitors,* 241

Brookner's seventeenth novel begins familiarly enough with a London setting. Its protagonist, however, finds her thoughts traveling to "gardens other than her own, gardens which were part of estates, demesnes, where richly endowed families conversed in idleness, sat on terraces, or awaited visitors. 'What meads, what *kvasses* were brewed, what pies were baked at Oblomovka!'"[11] The reference is to the 1859 Russian realist novel *Oblomov,* by Ivan Aleksandrovich Goncharov, which is about a passive and kindly aristocrat and a friend who is his total opposite in every way. Juxtapositions of this kind are frequently found in Brookner's novels, and *Visitors* is no exception. The same is true of *A Friend from England,* which also features this allusion in its first chapter with the words "What meads, what kvasses were drunk, what pies were baked at Oblomokov!" (24). This is the only repetition of its kind in all of Brookner's nineteen novels. It is also the only time that Russian is used—a *kvass* is an alcoholic beverage made from fermented rye flour. This is significant for several reasons. The most obvious is that it suggests a link between *Visitors* and *A Friend for England.* It foreshadows the juxtaposition between the protagonist, Dorothea

May, and her dead husband's cousin Kitty. It also is in keeping with Brookner's use of French in other novels which, with the slight exception of *Providence* and *Dolly,* is almost always part of a literary allusion. Since so many of her protagonists are writers, lecturers, librarians, or merely avid readers, literary allusions in any language never seem forced or contrived in these novels. Nonetheless, the introduction of even one foreign word (such as *kvass*) cannot go unnoticed, particularly given Brookner's refusal to embellish even her foreign settings with the sounds of other languages.

Just briefly looking at the contexts in which references to *Oblomov* occur in *A Friend from England* and *Visitors* reveals significant meaning. In the first, it contributes to the sense that the Livingstones were so unlike anyone Rachel had known that it was as if she were "in the presence of a distinct culture" (24). By equating them with nineteenth-century Russian aristocracy, Rachel's awe of her adopted "family" comes across. So too does her difference from them, and the inevitability that the world they offer to her will come to an end. In *Visitors,* the inspiration for this reference is a summer evening of incomparable light. This is not the first time that Brookner has loosed her art critic eye in a text. *The Misalliance* shows Blanche studying the light in a painting at the start of the novel, something that would evolve into a motif for her disaffection with life as it is and her wish for something different. Similarly, the protagonist of *Visitors* is less contented than she appears. At the start of the narrative, for example, the seventy-year-old Mrs. May is said to have "feared the dark, [and] welcomed the light . . . [which] provided a respite from bodily ills" (3). This particular summer evening, which is uncommonly warm and clear for London, makes her think of gardens and lives wholly unlike her own. Basically, this moment is a distraction, just as Steve Best's visit to her will take her mind, at least briefly, away from morbid thoughts.

The contrast between the garden onto which Mrs. May's apartment looks and the Russian one could not be greater. Whereas hers is empty, the latter is full of "families" and the refreshments associated with celebrations and other gatherings. By reducing the former to its falling light, Brookner sets the pattern for her most "stripped-down book" in which little happens at all beyond its protagonist's thoughts.[12] There are others besides this contrast between the liveliness of the garden that Mrs. May imagines and the quiet of her own. Whereas the protagonist of Goncharov's novel owns not only the garden but the entire village in which he lives, the garden that Mrs. May looks onto is a communal one for the residents of her apartment building. The impression that it is her own is broken when evening comes and she must close the French doors that lead from her apartment out to it. Leaving these doors open is one thing during the day, another at night. Mrs. May is not portrayed as foolhardy but hardier than almost everyone she knew who "seemed to be on guard against imaginary dangers" all of the time (5). Her imagination works differently. With her doors open onto this garden she could, for example, "imagine country emanations in the stillness of the early morning," although she is described as "a Londoner born and bred" (5). The distinction between what this protagonist is and what she would like to be is revealing. As the allusions to Goncharov's novel suggest, Edenic associations for Mrs. May not only require a pastoral setting but one that is distinctly not English. Here, as in all of Brookner's novels, settings abroad are equated with escape and happiness.

Another significant difference separating these gardens is that Mrs. May's is presented as real, whereas the others are the stuff of "novels and stories" (3). How the actual world and that depicted in literature differ has been the subject, to a greater or lesser extent, throughout Brookner's writing. Ever since Ruth in *The Debut,* numerous protagonists have been beset with the problem of distinguishing between the lessons of literature and the realities of life. Even in *Providence* where the novel Kitty is teaching so obviously parallels her own life, the difficulty for Brookner's protagonists can be in discerning when and how literature can be instructive.

The fact that the fiction that comes to Mrs. May's mind is Russian and not English is significant in several ways. It fits a pattern throughout Brookner's writing, in which settings rarely confine her characters for long. Whether physically or mentally, there is a journeying beyond London to Paris and Venice or, in this case, Oblomovka. Other English cities, let alone the English countryside or the rest of the British Isles, do not effectively exist. The resulting polarity (in literature and life) is one between the Englishness that London represents and the mystique of certain European cultures. Two such cultures dominate; French literature and a Paris setting feature with the greatest frequency in Brookner's writing, followed by more general allusions to Russian culture.

Nowhere in *Visitors* does Brookner state that Mrs. May or her late husband's family are Jewish. Their names, like their habits, give little away. But in pointing out that Mrs. May lives in Golders Green, a part of London with a predominantly Jewish population for many years, Brookner introduces a Jewish element into the novel from its first pages. This would explain Mrs. May's train of thought, which runs so freely from such disparate worlds as "that Russia" of presumably nineteenth-century fiction and contemporary London (3). The implication is that the former is a lost world, not merely an imaginary one. All of this is significant in foreshadowing events to come. For Mrs. May will in effect visit that world of families awaiting visitors, as the title *Visitors* suggests.

Ostensibly, however, Mrs. May sees only one journey ahead. That is the inevitable decline of old age. As a childless widow with no family except for some distant in-laws, Mrs. May is a particularly solitary figure. Yet this is not to say that she is presented as especially worse off than others her age. For one thing, this protagonist is totally devoid of self-pity. For another, she envisages this final journey—toward death—as a solitary affair whatever one's circumstances. Given that Mrs. May perceives physical deterioration as inevitable (her heart condition goes untreated as a result), the focus in the novel is on this protagonist's mental state. Thoughts about death and the possibility of an afterlife are conveyed through introspective passages that contribute to a view that aging is more significantly an emotional than a physical trial. Described as being "in a country without maps," the experience of aging is equated with going on a journey for which one is unprepared (234). In the absence of any guide, the onus for finding "some middle way, between acceptance and defeat" is on the individual (235). The mental processes that this involves are described in terms of traversing an urban landscape, which in the absence particularly of nature imagery, eliminates any suggestion of a pastoral ideal or Eden-like associations. By reducing this "journey" to the image of someone crossing a street, Brookner strips it of any romanticism, glamor, or conventional adventure. Instead, what comes to mind is the picture of an elderly person whose last vestige of independence is maintained by a daily walk to the shops, which "must be negotiated without assistance: that was the rule" (235).

Mrs. May arrives at these conclusions at the end of the novel, after the departure of her young houseguest. As with so many of Brookner's novels, this makes for a certain circularity in the narrative, as the protagonist is restored to her original solitary state. It also fits the pattern of many others in which revelations are arrived at when a relationship has ended. That the houseguest is male and attractive particularly invites comparisons to Brookner's early novels. How *Visitors* diverges from the pattern set in *Providence, Look at Me,* and others, however, has less to do with the considerable age difference separating Mrs. May from Steve than with the nature of their relationship and how it ends.

Unlike so many of Brookner's protagonists, Mrs. May does not *want* her solitude broken. This is made clear from the start in the narrative and in what she says to her visitor. Reminiscences about her late husband, Henry, also serve to reinforce an image of woman alone who prefers to be that way. For example, although she is described as having loved Henry, she "felt a sort of elation on realising that in the future she would not be disturbed" (85). On the surface, what Mrs. May does not want is a disruption of her quiet daily routines. But how Steve proves to be disturbing is in the way he makes Mrs. May's thoughts wander. These range from thoughts of her late husband and a lover in an illicit affair that ends tragically in suicide to the son she never had.

If Steve fails to come off the page as anything more than a "male presence," that is precisely because that is what he is to this novel's protagonist. Similarly, the male love interests in *The Debut, Providence, Look at Me,* and *Hotel du Lac* are not nearly as completely drawn as their female protagonists. Faulting Brookner on this account is to confuse the writer with her creation. If anyone is "to blame" it is the Ruth Weisses, Kitty Maules, etc, who perceive such diverse men as Professor Duplessis and Maurice Bishop solely in terms of how they function as lovers. Beyond that, their existence is only sketchily drawn in these texts, as it is in these protagonists' imaginations. In *Visitors,* Brookner takes this point even further. Steve is everyman to Mrs. May. As a result, he is superior to them all. Thus, she realizes that his departure will be altogether different from her husband's: "Clearing up his empty room would not provide that curious relief that she had felt when clearing Henry's room after his death" (86).

In a complete reversal of the downward turn that so often characterizes the male/female relationships in Brookner's novels, this one ends positively. In marked contrast to those in which protagonists are alone when they realize that their relationships have come to an end, Mrs. May and Steve are together. Unlike Maurice, who is more informed than Kitty in *Providence* or James as compared with Francis in *Look at Me,* these two are equally informed that Steve will be leaving. What is shocking is *how* he goes, and then the shock is one of pleasure. In a setting even more public than the dinner parties that prove so humiliating for the protagonists of *Providence* and *Look at Me,* a street is the setting for this denouement. The wedding party is sending off its bride and groom on their honeymoon as Steve suddenly makes Mrs. May the center of attention when, "bending her backwards he enfolded her in an elaborate Hollywood embrace" (204). To say (as one reviewer has) that there is "little that is fresh, in imaginative terms, in *Visitors*" is to overlook the significance of this scene.[13] For one thing, it is fun. Nothing could be in more marked contrast to the cruel spectacle of Alix piling her hair up to show off her slender neck before the brace- and wheelchair-bound Olivia in

Look at Me, or Hartman's horror at Fibich's breakdown in a restaurant in *Latecomers.* Secondly, this is the first time that a Brookner protagonist has everyone's attention for anything besides pity or possibly professional admiration, such as when Kitty gives her final lecture in *Providence.* Joy is rare enough in Brookner's novels. Here it is made triumphant by its public setting.

This scene also disproves the claim that *Visitors* is merely "a continuation of the novelist's design" in the way that it presents a departure from previous allusions to Hollywood movies.[14] Whereas in *Brief Lives* Fay is struck by how her life bears little resemblance to the romantic comedies she grew up watching, reality increasingly looks like something out of a movie to the protagonist of *Visitors.* Men are central in both cases but to different effect. Owen disappoints, whereas Steve reminds Mrs. May of matinee idols Ronald Coleman and Leslie Howard. "He must have seen old films on television," she conjectures after he puts on the charm one evening (127). On another occasion, his voice is described as having "the intonation from a wartime film" (182). When he jokes, "Darling, tell me I'm forgiven," his voice is called "actorish" (182). In each instance, the protagonist is pleased, and there is no indication in the narrative that she should have any reason to be otherwise. The decidedly positive context in which these Hollywood allusions arise is a dramatic change from what we have come to expect in Brookner's writing, although such associations may not in themselves be uncommon for someone of this protagonist's generation to make.

Just as a celluloid and actual reality appear to merge with Steve's visit, there is no great disparity between the fictional world alluded to at the start of the novel and the events that follow. For this reason, Mrs. May does not reject literature, as Ruth does in *The Debut.*

Briefly, at least, with the occasion of a distant relation's wedding, there is that splendor reminiscent of Russian novels in which families "awaited visitors" (3). If the hours that lead up to this wedding are not particularly eventful, that may be because the real event ahead for the protagonist of *Visitors* is the one that is to come. Her frequent ruminations about her own death make the anticipation and trepidation before the wedding effectively a prelude to that event. As a result, the former is of secondary importance to her mental state as she looks ahead to that future. However, it is presented as instructive. Concluding at the end of the text that "some form of solidarity was in order" when she embarks on that final journey, this wedding is likened to a prelude of events to come (241). In both, "help must be solicited and offered," she decides, and in so doing makes the most positive, though unsentimental, claim for family ties in perhaps all of Brookner's novels (241).

CHAPTER SEVEN

Back to the Beginning?
Falling Slowly and *Undue Influence*

Falling Slowly

Clearly it was safer and more prudent not to look in
windows, not to have access to other people's
worlds.

Falling Slowly, 8

Every country is home to one man
And exile to another.
    T. S. Eliot, "To the Indians Who Died in Africa"

Brookner's eighteenth novel appears to offer a break from the
relentlessness that has marked her previous seventeen. For the first
time, here is a protagonist who has a sibling. In contrast to the steady
stream of only children, frequently orphans, who populate Brookner's
novels, the presence of a sibling might suggest some relief from
loneliness, or even a study in healthy rivalry. Neither transpires in
Falling Slowly. The first image is of Miriam Sharpe looking for
"something to lift the spirits."[1] Rather than being a breather from the
solitude and introspective beating that Brookner has subjected her
protagonists to for nearly two decades, *Falling Slowly* has all the
hallmarks of these and more. What is so striking about this and
Undue Influence is how many echoes there are of her very earliest
novels—*The Debut, Providence, Look at Me,* and *Hotel du Lac*—all
of which have the romantic trials of a single female protagonist as
their focus.

To begin with, the introduction of Miriam before, and separate, from Beatrice makes one sister, more than the other, the focus of the novel. Instead of depicting the story of two sisters and their relationship to one another, this start to the novel suggests that Miriam, who will outlive her sister, is the true protagonist. This is in contrast to *Latecomers,* in which Fibich and Hartmann mirror one another's lives with no such separations. The image of Miriam solitarily looking "as usual" at the pictures in a gallery window also creates the impression that this is a protagonist who is frequently on her own (3). Being, like all of Brookner's protagonists, a creature of habit, the particular form her browsing takes also reveals someone who is rarely with others. The fact that she remains outside the galleries looking in suggests an outsider status that is supported in the text by her lack of connection to anyone, whether by marriage, friendship, or the merest social contact. By not entering the galleries, Miriam is presented as someone of vicarious pleasures. In the absence of physical engagement that entering the galleries might afford, for example to smell the canvases and paint, possibly touch a frame, or greet the proprietor with a word or handshake, even the protagonist's visual delight is reductive. This is supported by her unfulfilled hopes that she would "find the image she unconsciously sought" (3). Thus, not only does the glass separating Miriam from the pictures suggest something beyond her reach, but the way that her browsing, by its regularity, is ritualized also contributes to an impression of something never ending.

Two other factors give little hope that Miriam's search is not in vain. First, the protagonist seems not to know what precisely she is looking for or why. Second, her expectations far surpass what ordinarily is associated with a small art purchase. If anything, her wish to be lifted, transported, and have her everyday life transcended sounds more like the job for a prince on a white horse or a knight in shining armor. As is clear from *The Debut* on, these are in short supply.

Perhaps what is most disturbing at the start of *Falling Slowly* is what happens when Miriam actually does find "something to her taste" (3). After staring at it for "seven or eight minutes . . . unperturbed by the jostling passers-by who barely register in her consciousness," she leaves it there (4). None of Brookner's protagonists is ever short of a pound, or a French or Swiss franc for that matter. Without exception, they are people with inheritances, property, investments, not to mention a regular shopper's knowledge of Harrods' food aisles. Why not buy the picture? Its content might supply some clues.

The nineteenth-century painting, called *Place du Chatelet under Snow* and attributed to one Eugene Laloue, depicts a winter evening in Paris. The contrast to Miriam's own surroundings is obvious. Not only is the painted scene removed from her by time in years but also season. The opening of *Falling Slowly* is set in T. S. Eliot's "cruellest month."[2] In addition to being in April, Miriam's thoughts take a direction that invites comparisons to the opening stanzas of *The Waste Land* and the stirring of "memory and desire" associated with the season (63). Though long dead, Beatrice comes to Miriam's mind, and, with her, a chronicle of disappointment and failed love that comprises the narrative. Other allusions to Eliot arise from Miriam's fascination, above all, with the "yellow sky" in the painting, inviting parallels to "the yellow smoke that slides along the street, / Rubbing its back upon the window-panes" in the beginning of "The Love Song of J. Alfred Prufrock" and "the brown fog" that in *The Waste Land* evokes the opening lines from Baudelaire's "Poem 93" in *Fleurs du Mal* concerning Paris.[3] The color yellow,

which so "continued to draw the eye" of Brookner's protagonist,
thus alludes to a common detail in both literary and visual art medi-
ums of French symbolism. If this seems to be stretching a point,
consider this protagonist's background and interests. She is a translator of books from French into English and English into French.
She has a second home in Paris where she makes "brief but regular
visits" to the agency that employs her (4). She is described to have
had, when younger, "an amorphous love of the arts," which her
intentness in studying this painting corroborates (7). In addition, the
narrative of *Falling Slowly* shows more intrusions of Brookner-the-
art-historian than any of her novels since *The Misalliance*. In some
respects, the correlation that Blanche makes between the archetypal
nymphs in paintings and the figure of Sally is so pointed that its significance seems undeserving of further attention. In *Falling Slowly,*
Brookner uses a lighter hand.

Comparable to the pointillism employed by impressionist painters,
the result here is that such allusions carry more weight because of
their subtlety. For example, the picture that captures Miriam's gaze
the longest is in a gallery that specializes in art "for easy consumption" (3). Here, as ever, Brookner thwarts any impulse to ennoble
her protagonist early on or on account of education or background.
Thus she emerges as someone of discerning taste and sharp intellect
(mirrored in her last name "Sharpe"), but who also yearns for the
comfort of simple pleasures. Brookner's choice of the word "consumption" is highly significant. Whether gastronomic or sexual,
physical or emotional, appetites regularly serve as barometers to
understanding her characters. As her choice of painting to look at
reveals, Miriam's taste is for "what could be easily managed, just as
she appreciated work that was well within her grasp" (8). This was

not always so, however. How Miriam's desires are diminished, like the appetite of a woman far in advance of her years, is the subject of this novel.

Key to what is to come is found in this scene outside a London gallery. The painting is beyond Miriam's grasp. So too will other objects of desire be for this protagonist, who concludes that, "it was safer and more prudent not to look in windows, not to have access to other people's worlds" (8). The images Miriam finds so disturbing in the painting *Place du Chatelet* are those that should be most comforting. They are the depictions of people journeying home. The fact that Miriam is on her way to work, not home, and that it is the start, not the end, of the day is not the problem. What is distressing is how these images remind the protagonist that even at her day's close there will be no such "homecoming" or "homegoing" (5). The reason is there is no one to welcome her. She has no attachments such as that which the image of the mother and child so epitomizes in the painting. In *Falling Slowly,* as in *Hotel du Lac, home* "implies husband, children, order, [and] regular meals," which makes even the use of the word a misappropriation that this protagonist avoids.[4]

The implication from the series of thoughts that are prompted by this painting is that without another's affirmation there can be no belonging. As a result, Miriam sees herself as being set apart from the figures in the painting, who have the confidence "not to wonder at their surroundings, not to be disconcerted by the bad weather and the fading light, and protected by that flag" (5). Never one for repetition, Brookner twice directs attention to what attracts Miriam's gaze. The yellow sky is not empty but holds a flag. Brookner is also not given to coining new words, yet here again she does just that with the word "homegoing" (5). Each of these factors points to a significance beyond the plotless start to this novel. For this painting, which is meant for "easy consumption," makes this protagonist feel uneasy. Instead of merely bringing to mind the comforts of home, it spins her into a reverie in which more questions are raised than are easily answered. One of these questions is, "whether a library, any library, was a way out or a way in" (5).

The parallels to Miriam's looking into the gallery windows and onto the lives of the figures with homes to go to in a French painting are fairly obvious. It would be mistaken, though, to assume that France is what lures her. "Paris held no secrets for her," Brookner writes (4). The foreign setting merely contributes to a sense that the contented life is exotic for this protagonist. The flag, because of its associations with nationhood, citizenship, and cultural identity, serves thus as a symbol for the cohesiveness of the community presented in the painting. On the outside looking in, Miriam's stance at the start of the novel foreshadows the marginalized existence that characterizes her entire life.

Exile is a recurring theme in Brookner's writing. The sense of tragedy that this is the case for Brookner's protagonists, however, had been played down in the novels she was writing in the 1990s. Her return so emphatically to this theme in the opening pages of *Falling Slowly* suggests a return to the concerns of her earlier novels. Particularly since this novel features a single female protagonist and her relations with men, the form and format of Brookner's first four novels comes especially to mind. What, however, are we to make of Beatrice? The existence of a sibling would appear at first glance to offer a respite from the isolation that is so commonly the bane of these protagonists' lives. As the narrative unfolds, more similarities than differences emerge between Brookner's eighteenth novel and *The Debut, Providence, Look at Me,* and *Hotel du Lac.*

BACK TO THE BEGINNING?

From the start of the novel, Beatrice is dead. Beatrice is also dead long before she crosses a street for a carton of milk and is struck by a car. In terms of career, she ceases to exist from the moment her agent's handsome young successor breaks the news that she is no longer on their books. Never a solo pianist but an accompanist, Beatrice has no professional future on her own. The correlation between Beatrice's career and personal aspirations is obvious. Totally without guile, Beatrice is a woman who "entered a room with a helpless suppliant air, as if looking for a pair of broad shoulders, of strong arms to which she might entrust her evident womanliness" (15). Forsaken by her agent Max when he retires to Monaco only to be discarded by his young successor Simon Haggard, Beatrice is presented as an innocent victim of displacement, as her sister recounts her life from chapter 2 onwards.

Although only middle-aged, Beatrice succumbs to retirement without ever once considering embarking on another career. Second chances, whether professional or personal, are rarely an option for Brookner's protagonists, with the possible exception of her male ones—Lewis Percy, Fibich and Hartmann in *Latecomers,* and George Bland in *A Private View*. Beatrice is thus reduced to an unwitting spectacle of her former self. In piled-high hair and long skirts, her appearance is that of the eternal accompanist waiting to go on stage. Yet unlike Miss Havisham who sits in her wedding dress in *Great Expectations,* Beatrice holds on to her belief in romance. As the older sister, Beatrice might be expected to advise Miriam, as Dickens's Miss Havisham does Stella. Here, however, Miriam is the one without romantic illusions, who tries to turn Beatrice around to her way of thinking. Both fail, in the characteristic way that Brookner's protagonists rarely ever act, but are acted upon. The catalyst for change is the same young agent who cancels Beatrice's contract. The swiftness with which Miriam takes up with Simon (literally as she shows him to the door after he has delivered the fatal blow to Beatrice) is faintly shocking.

In looks and manner, Simon fits the bill of the dashing suitor. The irony is that the sister without faith, even in the existence of such a prince, should be the one to be swept off her feet. Biblical allusions to the coming of a messiah are delicately drawn here. Brookner, who says she is not "a believer," though raised Jewish, appears at first to be reworking the parable of the virgins with lamps who wait for the coming of Jesus.[5] The one without faith seems to reap the rewards. As it turns out, however, Simon Haggard is no savior. Married, egotistical, and without conscience, he effectively robs Miriam of her heart when their affair ends. The tragedy is that when her real rescuer comes in the form of Tom Rivers, she is still sold on the former.

Impostors are a frequent feature in Brookner's writing; Simon belongs to the club, but through no fault of his own. Miriam knows full well that he has a wife and children. No charges of bigamy could even remotely be raised here, in contrast to George Ainsworth's crime against Amy Durrant in *Fraud*. This one does not even bandy about the words "my love," as Maurice Bishop does in *Providence*. In retrospect, Edith's David is a better catch in *Hotel du Lac*. At least he appears to feel *something* when he learns of her impending marriage to Geoffrey Long. All that can be said about Simon is that he is good-looking and makes love to Miriam. In these respects, at least, he does not fail her. That comes when she expects him to be true to her.

Mistresses have no rights. The parallel between women in such a predicament and persons displaced by war or other catastrophic events comes from the lack of protection that both suffer. Lacking any claim to the men who take their affection, mistresses are the quintessential outsider. Their lack of belonging is comparable to a form of statelessness. Thus, the French painting that so captures Miriam's attention at the start of the novel is, with its images of families and flags, both alluring and disturbing for this protagonist. She surmises that looking in windows or onto other people's lives can be risky. You not only end up wanting more. You find yourself with less. As one reviewer puts it, "there is no pretence . . . that less is more. Less is less" in this novel.[6] The words "falling slowly" are the last in the predawn shipping forecast on British radio. They mark the end of one day and the start of another. *Falling* in love similarly promises a transformation. What Miriam had forgotten is the fate that befalls mortals who fall for gods.

Undue Influence

> Working in a bookshop makes one acquainted with
> titles rather than texts.
>
> *Undue Influence,* 15–16

Brookner's writing has been called "close to perfection."[7] At the start of *Undue Influence,* it would seem that she is placing the single flaw in an otherwise perfect Persian carpet. The same "elegance and precision" that we have come to expect is there in every sentence, but their message is that this novel's protagonist is deeply flawed.[8]

Brookner's protagonists are generally a smart lot. They read books. They even write books. In *Undue Influence,* Claire Pitt sells them. She also lives surreptitiously through other people, as if their lives were as accessible as the books that surround her. The problem is that she treats people as she does books. "Working in a bookshop makes one acquainted with titles rather than texts," she says.[9] "In fact I read very little" (15). Like the books in the shop where she works, people are known to this protagonist only on a surface level. Herein lies the problem. Just as covers can be deceptive, so too can the images people project of themselves. This hardly matters if the books remain on the shelves, or the people whom she observes remain passersby on the street. There are consequences, however, should one decide to take either home. This is just what Claire Pitt does. *Undue Influence* is the story of a twenty-nine-year-old shop clerk who falls in love with one of her customers. Before taking him home to bed with her, she gets "closer" to him by her self-confessed fascination with constructing people's lives for herself (15). Calling herself "a mental stalker," the implication is that others are subjected to her whims not the other way around (15). The person who is stalked, not the stalker, is, after all, the one conventionally looked upon as the victim. Yet Claire Pitt, not Martin Gibson, is the injured party in this affair. As with *Falling Slowly,* echoes of ill-fated romances for single young female protagonists in *The Debut, Providence, Look at Me,* and *Hotel du Lac* suggest that Brookner is returning to the concerns and scenarios of her early work.

In a clever twist of the opening of *The Debut,* in which we learn Ruth Weiss's belief that "her life had been ruined by literature," *Undue Influence* begins with Claire Pitt telling us a story. The significance of the latter is in foreshadowing another story that will be ruinous to her. The irony that makes this ruin so tragic is that the protagonist of *Undue Influence* is the reader *and* the author of both stories. In this regard, Claire Pitt resembles *Providence*'s Kitty Maule, who similarly misconstrues the actions of the man whom she adores.

The result in both novels is a fiction created by these protagonists that bears little relation to reality, serving instead to mock the disparity between their hopes and lack of fulfillment. Worse off even than the protagonists of *The Debut, Look at Me,* and *Hotel du Lac,* Claire Pitt, like Kitty Maule, can only blame herself.

The opening chapter of *Undue Influence* ends with the ominous words, "It was not the first time I had been guilty of a misapprehension" (7). These conclude the story of an upstairs neighbor whom the protagonist had grossly misjudged. With scant information and an imagination that runs to stereotypes (the domineering mother, the submissive son), Claire constructs a scenario that falls far short of the truth. The mother, not the son, is in fact the victim of events. Described as, "one more old lady submitting to the inevitable shipwreck," emotional turmoil is equated with disasters of Titanic proportions (6). Mrs. Hildreth, who is spurned by her son for a new wife, has the air of someone whose days "were nearly over" (6). What is foreshadowed, of course, is the demise of the novel's protagonist who will similarly be spurned for another woman by the man she loves.

Initially, however, her interpretation of her upstairs neighbors' "ferocious altercation" sounds wholly plausible (3). Recounting how she pieced together the events of that night, one is reminded of Sir Arthur Conan Doyle's stories, both in her sleuthing genius for deducing so much from so little and in the elegant restraint of the sentences that never succumb to dramatizing events, but exhibit a detached control at all times. As a result of these impressions, the mistakenness of her surmising, comes as a surprise. The reason for this is simple. Like so many of Brookner's protagonists, Claire Pitt is not unintelligent. Domineering mothers do exist. So do submissive sons. But lacking "the information," as Kitty Maule puts it at the end of *Providence,* a fiction as easily as the truth can be assembled (182).

This is the first of many similarities between *Undue Influence* and *Providence.* Others include the youthfulness of the protagonist. At a time when Brookner's protagonists seemed to have been aging with her, Claire is just twenty-nine. Like Kitty, she is an only child who has lost both parents and has few connections to anyone else. Her only friend (comparable to Kitty's colleague Pauline) is more self-assured and knowledgeable about events than she is. In *Providence,* it is not far-fetched to imagine that Pauline could have made Kitty better informed about Maurice's activities. In *Undue Influence,* Claire's friend Wiggy unwittingly is the one who breaks the news of Martin's unfaithfulness to her. In both novels, a romantic interest is the focus that captivates and torments the protagonist. Like Maurice, Martin is English, upper-class, well-off, and handsome to the point of being "iconic" (35). In neither text is the word "love" ever used by the protagonists to express their feelings for these men. Nonetheless, their desire for inhabiting the worlds these men represent is unmistakable. Their adoration of these men is as all-consuming as religious ecstasy, though neither has any faith in such things, in contrast, for example, to Maurice, who is a devout Catholic. Firm rationalists, both protagonists believe in order and connection. "There are no accidents," believes Claire (49). When the protagonists in both novels discover that these men's affections are directed elsewhere, feelings of humiliation and rejection are devastating.

If the story line of *Undue Influence* sounds familiar, so too are the philosophical questions that Brookner returns to seventeen years after they were first introduced in *The Debut.* These concern matters of duty and free will. Isaac Bashevis Singer has said, "You cannot write a love story of two human beings without dealing with their background—what nation they belonged to, what language their fathers spoke at home, and where they grew up."[10] In *Undue Influence,* Brookner follows suit. The narrative concerns Claire's life before Martin and Martin's life before Claire. The problem is that Claire has to be relied on for both, and her narratorial authority has already been undermined in chapter 1. The problem is not a lack of honesty, but information that should make us wary of Claire's version of events. As a result, any accounts of Martin's life beyond his sexual relations with Claire cannot be trusted. Rather than setting out to uncover mysteries, she fills in the missing details through conjecture. When Edith Hope does this in *Hotel du Lac,* the result is humorous. Mrs. Pusey is much older and her daughter much wiser than they first seemed, etc. Even Edith's discovery that Neville is sleeping with the latter is not as grave as when Claire learns that Martin has been seeing his invalid wife's former nurse. The reason for this is simple. Edith has her married lover to return to. Claire has no one.

When Claire's mother dies, her friend Wiggy's first words to her are, "It's you who are free now. Will you make any changes, do you think?" (15). Coming from someone who would seem to epitomize powerlessness (Wiggy has been the mistress of a married man for years), advice on empowerment might seem absurd. But a brief look at the these two characters indicates otherwise. Little is known about Wiggy except that she is devoted to her lover and happy to be so. Claire, on the other hand, who has acted with devotion by caring for her invalid mother and father for years, is a figure of discontentment. Having no belief in an afterlife, Claire is nonetheless plagued by the

memories of those years. The image of her father masturbating beneath his hospital gown brutally conveys her revulsion towards him.
For her mother, she feels mostly pity. Wiggy, who knows the devotion that goes with love, assumes that Claire is now freed by their
deaths to pursue the love of a man.

But just as Claire is not wholly a loving daughter, she has not
exactly been putting her life on hold. In fact, she has been leading
another life altogether, a sexually liberated one in France. Double
lives, or secret ones, were first a major feature in *Providence,* followed
by *Hotel du Lac*. In the latter especially, the issue of freedom and its
merits is raised when Edith defends romance writing because it fills
a public desire for the old myths, something comparable to the meek
inheriting the earth. Feminism has many shortcomings in Edith's
view, otherwise if the modern woman is "all that liberated, why
doesn't she go down to the bar and pick someone up?" (27). Every
implication is that Claire does just that. Yet she is not happy.
Toward the end of *Undue Influence,* she discloses what may be the
reason why. "Now let me tell you what a woman wants," she begins,
imagining that Martin were listening (195). "A woman wants . . .
ardour, an erotic eagerness that goes beyond the physical. The desire
and pursuit of the whole. And also an unmasking, so that it will
become possible to meet on every level" (186). It is a tall order, one
that sex alone falls far short of fulfilling.

In the absence of a relationship that is as intimate spiritually as
physically, Claire unmasks herself to the reader, saying that her holidays "are not spent exclusively in French provincial towns looking
at cathedrals, although such towns are as amendable to adventures
as any other place" (10). This is Brookner at her understated best. In
place of details of the "adventures" that make this good girl so bad,

a list of cathedrals follows: "It is enough for me to entertain my mother on my return from Chartres or Amiens or Bourges or Strasbourg with an account of the byways of the town visited, and with the photographs and postcards to prove that I was there, to make me feel straightforward, reconnected with her worthiness in a way that has been mislaid from time to time. Besides, I like French cathedrals, although not perhaps the flashier ones. Vienne and Autun are more to my taste than Troyes, although Troyes has a lot going for it. Le Mans was the only dead end: Dijon came close. Coutances was pleasant" (10–11). This passage appears at first to tell more about Claire's deception of her mother than her sexual exploits abroad. On a second reading, however, more can be discerned. The listing of cathedrals provides a route of sorts in which the map of France is crisscrossed from north to south, east to west. This configuration is not far removed from a cross, which is a reminder that cathedrals are Claire's proposed purpose for these trips. Yet, knowing that this is primarily a pretense for sexual escapades, the intersection of lines also brings to mind other intersections, or "joinings," to which Claire has previously alluded.

The language she uses to describe the cathedrals supports a reading of this passage as a highly codified description of sexual adventures. From the words "Besides, I like French cathedrals" the tone is anything but elevated (11). The word "flashier," although not limited to this use, is more often applied to people and cars. References to "taste," just as to appetites and food in general, are too commonly associated with sexuality in Brookner's novels to ignore here, particularly given this protagonist's admitted promiscuity. The proliferation of idiomatic expressions ("to my taste," "a lot going for it," "dead end," and "came close") in these sentences is at variance with this narrator's style, something that indicates a significance beyond what may be obvious.

Accustomed to disguise, not disclosure, the narrator employs the former to recount her adventures. The names of cathedrals might thus take the place of her lovers' names (which she may not even remember given their number and unimportance). The fact that cathedrals by definition house bishops supports the connection of place with persons (male), and church ritual with performance (sexual), and the spiritual with sensual experience. In *Providence,* Brookner develops these links even further by giving Maurice the last name "Bishop." Although his cathedral tour with Kitty does not take him into her bed, the implication afterwards is that this is because he has been with Miss Fairchild. Here, as in the ending of *Undue Influence,* the allusions and parallels to *Providence* point to Brookner's return to her first novels' focus on love, mystery, and belonging.

The shock at the end of *Undue Influence,* when Claire learns that Martin and his deceased wife's nurse are a couple, is especially reminiscent of the end of *Providence.* Since the reader is no more informed than either protagonist, these final scenes are shocking in spite of Brookner's refusal to embellish them. Comparable to her protagonists who in *Providence* must converse over dinner or in *Undue Influence* must finish a telephone call, Brookner continues as ever in a style that is controlled in spite of her protagonists' lack of it. Witnessing how Kitty Maule and Claire Pitt do not let their masks fall is thus a painful yet inspiring vision. For these protagonists do not, in these moments, merely stand alone. They also stand tall. Comparable to the painting *The Execution of Lady Jane Gray* in front of which Claire and Wiggy become friends in London's National Gallery,

Undue Influence ends in failure but no loss of dignity for its protagonist. Like Lady Gray in "her best dress," Claire Pitt and her predecessors make "a lasting impression" more truly iconic than the men they adored (11). Perhaps here as in *Falling Slowly,* Brookner's return is not only to reworking features of her first novels, but also to her love of art history. Time will tell if the significance of paintings in these last novels of the 1990s heralds a new direction for Brookner, in which her skills as a novelist and art historian are brought to the fore. Whatever its form, Brookner's dark aesthetic is a thing of beauty.

NOTES

Chapter 1—Understanding Anita Brookner

1. Shusha Guppy, "Interview: The Art of Fiction XCVII: Anita Brookner," *Paris Review* 109 (1987): 150.

2. Guppy, "Interview," 148–49.

3. John Haffenden, "Anita Brookner," in *Novelists in Interview,* ed. John Haffenden (London and New York: Methuen, 1985), 63.

4. Haffenden, "Anita Brookner," 68.

5. Brookner, *Hotel du Lac* (New York: Pantheon, 1984), 23. Page references in parentheses are to this edition.

6. Guppy, "Interview," 149.

7. Guppy, "Interview," 149.

8. Haffenden, "Anita Brookner," 64.

9. Robert E. Hosmer, "Anita Brookner," in *Dictionary of Literary Biography Yearbook 1987,* ed. J. M. Brook (Detroit: Gale Bruccoli Clark Layman, 1988), 297.

10. Kate Fulbrook, "Anita Brookner," in *Dictionary of Literary Biography: British Novelists since 1960,* ed. Merritt Moseley (Detroit: Gale Bruccoli Clark Layman, 1998), 39.

11. Fulbrook, "Anita Brookner," 42.

12. Joyce Carol Oates, "Writing for the Tortoise Market," review of *Undue Influence, Times Literary Supplement,* 30 July 1999, 19.

13. John Skinner, *The Fictions of Anita Brookner: Illusions of Romance* (London: Macmillan, 1992), 2.

14. Angela McRobbie, "Fine Disorder," review of *Hotel du Lac, New Statesman,* 7 Sept. 1984, 34.

15. Pascale Frey, "Comment Rater Sa Vie," review of *Incidents in the Rue Laugier, Lire,* Oct. 1995, 23.

16. Brian Cheyette, ed., *Contemporary Jewish Writing in Britain and Ireland: An Anthology* (Lincoln: University of Nebraska Press, 1998), xxxv.

17. Elie Wiesel, review of *The Shawl,* by Cynthia Ozick, *Chicago Tribune Books,* 17 Sept. 1989, 6.

18. Ibid.

19. Alan L. Berger, *Crisis and Covenant: The Holocaust in American Jewish Fiction* (Albany: State University of New York Press, 1985), 33.

20. 1 Ezek. 33:10, quoted in Berger, *Crisis and Covenant,* 39.

21. Cynthia Ozick, *The Shawl* (New York: Vintage, 1989), 19.

22. Brookner, "O for the Voice to be Still," review of *The Oracle at Stoneleigh Court,* by Peter Taylor, *Spectator,* 6 Mar. 1993, 26.

23. Brookner, "Hamlet, Thought Not Meant to Be," review of *The Prince of West End Avenue,* by Alan Isler, *Spectator,* 4 Feb. 1995, 29.

24. Brookner, "An Escape but More Than Escapism," review of *Ladder of Years,* by Anne Tyler, *Spectator,* 29 Apr. 1995, 35.

25. Brookner, "A Nun of Art," review of *Judith Gautier: A Biography,* by Joanna Richardson, *Times Literary Supplement,* 6 Mar. 1987, 236.

26. Brookner, *Hotel du Lac* (New York: Pantheon, 1984), 28. Page references in parentheses are to this edition,

27. Guppy, "Interview," 157.

28. Brookner, "In the Incomparable Spaces," review of the exhibit *François Boucher, 1703–1770, Spectator,* 10 Oct. 1986, 1137.

29. Brookner, "Looking Back in Sorrow," review of *Memories of the Ford Administration,* by John Updike, *Spectator,* 27 Feb. 1993, 30.

30. Ibid.

31. Haffenden, "Anita Brookner," 72.

32. Brookner, "A Superb Achievement," review of *The Unconsoled,* by Kazuo Ishiguro, *Spectator,* 24 June 1995, 40.

33. Ann Fisher-Wirth, "Hunger Art: The Novels of Anita Brookner," *Twentieth Century Literature,* 41, no. 1 (1995): 1.

Chapter 2—Can't Buy Me Love: *The Debut, Providence, Look at Me,* and *Hotel du Lac*

1. Hosmer, "Anita Brookner," 294.

2. Guppy, "Interview," 150.

3. Haffenden, "Anita Brookner," 60.

4. Ibid., 66.

5. Brookner, *The Debut* (*A Start in Life*) (1981; reprint, New York: Vintage Contemporaries, 1990), 7. Page references in parentheses are to this edition.

6. Mary Anne Schofield, "Spinster's Fare: Rites of Passage in Anita Brookner's Fiction," in *Cooking by the Book: Food in Literature and Culture,* ed. Mary Anne Schofield (Bowling Greene: Bowling Greene State University Popular Press, 1989), 63.

7. David Galef, "You Aren't What You Eat: Anita Brookner's Dilemma," *Journal of Popular Culture* 28, no. 3 (1994): 2.

8. Ibid.

9. Fisher-Wirth, "Hunger Art," 4.

10. Brookner, *Providence* (1982; reprint, New York: Vintage Contemporaries, 1990), 182. Page references in parentheses are to this edition.

11. Arthur Marwick, *British Society since 1945* (Harmondsworth: Penguin, 1982), 38–39.

12. Brookner, *Look at Me* (1983; reprint, New York: E. P. Dutton, 1985), 11. Page references in parentheses are to this edition.

13. Alastair Niven, *Contemporary British Novelists,* poster series produced by the British Council (London, 1989).

14. Gaby Wood, "An Elegant Muteness," review of *Incidents in the Rue Laugier, Times Literary Supplement,* 2 June 1995, 750.

15. "Nation," *The New Shorter Oxford English Dictionary.*

16. Olga Kenyon, *Women Novelists Today: A Survey of English Writing in the Seventies and Eighties* (Brighton: Harvester, 1988), 12.

17. E. M. Forster, *Aspects of the Novel* (1927; reprint, Harmondsworth: Penguin, 1962), 60–61.

18. 1 Sam. 16:7.

Chapter 3—What Child Is This . . . : *Family and Friends, The Misalliance, A Friend from England,* and *Latecomers*

1. Brookner, *Family and Friends* (1985; reprint, New York: Pocket Books, 1986), 19. Page references in parentheses are to this edition.

2. A. N. Wilson, "Significant Silences," review of *Family and Friends, Times Literary Supplement,* 6 Sept. 1985, 973.

3. Guppy, "Interview," 153.

4. Ibid.

5. Brookner, "A Servant or a Saint," review of *The Good Husband,* by Gail Godwin, *Spectator,* 5 Nov. 1994, 51.

6. Gayle Greene, *Changing the Story: Feminist Fiction and Tradition* (Bloomington: Indiana University Press, 1991), 200.

7. Brookner, *The Misalliance* (1986; reprint, New York: Perennial, 1988), 1. Page references in parentheses are to this edition.

8. Skinner, *The Fictions of Anita Brookner,* 104.

9. Guppy, "Interview," 166.

10. Ibid.

11. Ibid., 167.

12. Brookner, *A Friend from England* (1987: reprint, New York: Perennial, 1989), 157. Page references in parentheses are to this edition.

13. Guppy, "Interview," 204.

14. Brookner, *Latecomers* (1988; reprint, New York: Vintage Contemporaries, 1988), 248. Page references in parentheses are to this edition.

15. Brian Cheyette, "Ineffable and Usable: Towards a Diasporic British-Jewish Writing," *Textual Practice* 10.2 (1996), 295, citing Phil Cohen, *Home Rules: Some Reflections on Racism and Nationalism in Everyday Life* (London: University of London Press, 1993), 34.

16. Carole Boyce Davies, *Black Women, Writing, and Identity: Migrations of the Subject* (New York: Routledge, 1994), 113.

17. Kobena Mercer, "1968: Periodizing Politics and Identity," in *Cultural Studies,* ed. Lawrence Grossberg, Cary Nelson, and Paula A. Treichler (New York: Routledge, 1992), 424.

18. Bernard Lewis, *Semites and Anti-Semites: An Inquiry into Conflict and Prejudice* (New York: Norton, 1986), 27.

Chapter 4—Happily Ever After? *Lewis Percy, Brief Lives,* and *A Closed Eye*

1. Skinner, *The Fictions of Anita Brookner*, 163.

2. Brookner, *Lewis Percy* (1989; reprint, New York: Pantheon, 1991), 76. Page references in parentheses are to this edition.

3. Skinner, *The Fictions of Anita Brookner*, 151.

4. Brookner, *Brief Lives* (1990; reprint, New York: Vintage Contemporaries, 1992), 15. Page references in parentheses are to this edition.

5. Lindsay Duguid, "The Downward Drag and the Loss of Allure," review of *Brief Lives*, by Anita Brookner, *Times Literary Supplement*, 24–30 Aug. 1990, 889.

6. Galef, "You Aren't What You Eat," 2.

7. Brookner, *A Closed Eye* (1991; reprint, New York: Vintage Contemporaries, 1993), 201. Page references in parentheses are to this edition.

Chapter 5—Starting Over: *Fraud, Dolly,* and *A Private View*

1. John Bayley, "Living with a Little Halibut," review of Fraud, by Anita Brookner, *London Review of Books*, 8 Oct. 1992, 12.

2. Ibid.

3. Brookner, *Fraud* (New York: Random House, 1992), 129. Page references in parentheses are to this edition.

4. Candice Rodd, "Drawing-Room Despair," review of *Fraud*, by Anita Brookner, *Times Literary Supplement*, 21 Aug. 1992, 17.

5. Charles Dickens, *A Tale of Two Cities* (London: Hazell, Watson & Viney, n.d.), 9.

6. Charles Dickens, *Little Dorrit* (1857; Harmondsworth: Penguin, 1973), 895.

7. Brookner, *Dolly* (New York: Random House, 1993). Page references in parentheses are to this edition.

8. Gerda Charles, "The Lot of the Single Woman," review of *Family and Friends*, *Jewish Chronicle*, 27 Sept. 1985, 9.

9. Gerda Charles, "Darkness and Light," review of *Dolly* (A Family Romance), *Jewish Chronicle*, 10 Sept. 1993, 63.

10. A. N. Wilson, "Significant Silences," review of *Family and Friends, Times Literary Supplement,* 6 Sept. 1985, 973.

11. Jonathan Yardley, "Worlds of Understanding," review of *Dolly* (*A Family Romance*), *Washington Post,* 20 Feb. 1994, 20.

12. Brookner, *A Private View* (New York: Random House, 1994), 3. Page references in parentheses are to this edition.

Chapter 6—Journeying to the End: *Incidents in the Rue Laugier, Altered States,* and *Visitors*

1. Brookner, *Incidents in the Rue Laugier* (New York: Random House, 1995), 3. Page references in parentheses are to this edition.

2. Jeanette Winterson, *The Passion* (1987; reprint, London: Vintage, 1996), 13, 160.

3. Heather Mallick, "Depressive Tale Lacks Substance," review of *Falling Slowly, Toronto Sun,* 6 Sept. 1998, http://www.canoe.ca/Jam-BooksReviews/sep6_brookner.html.

4. Ibid.

5. Emily Giesler, "Brookner's Novel Fails to Compare to Jane Austen," review of *Incidents in the Rue Laugier, Maneater,* 2 Feb. 1996, http://www.maneater.com.

6. Giesler, "Brookner's Novel Fails to Compare to Jane Austen."

7. Guppy, "Interview," 151.

8. Ibid.

9. Brookner, *Altered States* (New York: Vintage Contemporaries, 1996), 6. Page references in parentheses are to this edition.

10. Guppy, "Interview," 152.

11. Brookner, *Visitors* (New York: Vintage Contemporaries, 1997), 241. Page references in parentheses are to this edition.

12. Jacqueline Carey, "Bleak House," review of *Visitors, New York Times Book Review,* 18 Jan. 1998, 10.

13. Sarah A. Smith, "Learnt from Life," review of *Visitors, Times Literary Supplement,* 39 May 1997, 21.

14. Smith, "Learnt from Life," 21.

Chapter 7—Back to the Beginning? *Falling Slowly* and *Undue Influence*

1. Brookner, *Falling Slowly* (New York: Vintage Contemporaries, 1998), 3. Page references in parentheses are to this edition.

2. T. S. Eliot, *The Waste Land, Collected Poems, 1909–1962,* (1963; reprint, London: Faber, 1975), line 1.

3. T. S. Eliot, "The Love Song of J. Alfred Prufrock," *Collected Poems, 1909–1962,* line 16, and *The Waste Land,* line 61.

4. Haffenden, "Anita Brookner," 71.

5. Guppy, "Interview," 149.

6. Gabriele Adnan, "Making the Best of It," review of *Falling Slowly,* by Anita Brookner, *Spectator,* 20 June 1998, 35.

7. Jonathan Yardley, "Worlds of Understanding," review of *Dolly* (*A Family Romance*), *Washington Post,* reprint, *Guardian Weekly,* 20 Feb. 1994, 20.

8. Michiko Kakutani, "Books of the Times," review of *Providence, New York Times,* 1 Feb. 1984, 23.

9. Brookner, *Undue Influence* (New York: Random House, 1999), 15–16. Page references in parentheses are to this edition.

10. Isaac Bashevis Singer and Richard Bruin, *Conversations with Isaac Bashevis Singer* (New York: Summit, 1985), 162.

BIBLIOGRAPHY

Works by Anita Brookner

A Start in Life. London: Cape, 1981. Republished as *The Debut*. New York: Linden, 1981.

Providence. London: Cape, 1982. New York: Pantheon, 1984.

Look at Me. London: Cape, 1983. New York: Pantheon, 1983.

Hotel du Lac. London: Cape, 1984. New York: Pantheon, 1984.

Family and Friends. London: Cape, 1985. New York: Pantheon, 1985.

A Misalliance. London: Cape, 1986. Republished as *The Misalliance*. New York: Pantheon, 1986.

A Friend from England. London: Cape, 1987. New York: Pantheon, 1987.

Latecomers. London: Cape, 1988. New York: Pantheon, 1988.

Lewis Percy. London: Cape, 1989. New York: Pantheon, 1989.

Brief Lives. London: Cape, 1990. New York: Random House, 1990.

A Closed Eye. London: Cape, 1991. New York: Random House, 1991.

Fraud. London: Cape, 1992. New York: Random House, 1992.

A Family Romance. London: Cape, 1993. Republished as *Dolly*. New York: Random House, 1993.

A Private View. London: Cape, 1994. New York: Random House, 1994.

Incidents in the Rue Laugier. London: Cape, 1995. New York: Random House, 1996.

Altered States. London: Cape, 1996. New York: Random House, 1996.

Visitors. London: Cape, 1997. New York: Random House, 1998.

Falling Slowly. London: Viking, 1998. New York: Random House, 1998.

Undue Influence. London: Viking, 1999. New York: Random House, 1999.

BIBLIOGRAPHY

Selected Works about Brookner

Books

Sadler, Lynn Veach. *Anita Brookner*. Boston: Twayne, 1990. Still useful for an introduction to Brookner's early work.

Skinner, John. *The Fictions of Anita Brookner: Illusions of Romance*. New York: St. Martin's, 1992. A perceptive analysis of the critical reception of Brookner's novels and its "growing polarization." Close readings of her first nine novels reveal the complex and extensive use Brookner makes of literary allusions, particularly from French literature.

Articles and Parts of Books

Fisher-Wirth, Ann. "Hunger Art: The Novels of Anita Brookner." *Twentieth Century Literature* 41, no. 1 (1995): 1–15. Fisher-Wirth argues that "nice girls finish last" in Brookner's novels because "allegiances are always to the phallocentric order" that "always rejects and betrays them."

Galef, David. "You Aren't What You Eat: Anita Brookner's Dilemma." *Journal of Popular Culture* 28, no. 3 (1994): 1–7. Food as an emblem, "indicative of love and yet a poor substitute for it," is a recurring motif from *The Debut* to *Lewis Percy,* proving that fixations about food like love are "hardly a female monopoly" in Brookner's writing.

Hosmer, Robert E., Jr. "Paradigm and Passage: The Fiction of Anita Brookner." In *Contemporary British Women Writers: Narrative Strategies,* edited by Robert E. Hosmer, Jr., 26–54. New York: St. Martin's, 1993. Hosmer argues convincingly that the Brookner's protagonists are figures of exile and outcast from Eden.

Kenyon, Olga. "Anita Brookner and the Woman's Novel." In *Women Novelists Today: A Survey of English Writing in the Seventies and*

BIBLIOGRAPHY

Eighties, 144–65. Brighton: Harvester, 1988. Focusing chiefly on *Hotel du Lac,* Kenyon contends that Brookner is a "post feminist" writer of romantic fiction.

Malcolm, Cheryl Alexander. "Compromise and Cultural Identity: British and American Perspectives in Anita Brookner's *Providence* and Cynthia Ozick's 'Virility.'" *English Studies* 78, no. 5 (1997): 459–71. This comparative essay defines Brookner's crucial issues to be assimilation, English identity, and the lot of the outsider.

Stetz, Margaret Diane. "Anita Brookner: Woman Writer as Reluctant Feminist." In *Writing the Woman Artist: Essays on Poetics, Politics, and Portraiture,* edited by Suzanne W. Jones, 96–112. Philadelphia: University of Pennsylvania Press, 1991. Stetz takes issue with Brookner's professed antifeminism, claiming she is "aesthetically feminist" in the depiction of mother-daughter relationships.

Interviews

Haffenden, John. "Anita Brookner." In *Novelists in Interview,* edited by John Haffenden, 57–84. London and New York: Methuen, 1985.

Guppy, Shusha. "Interview: The Art of Fiction XCVII: Anita Brookner." *Paris Review* 109 (1987): 146–69.

INDEX

AEF-8686